P9-BYU-661

chop

chop

expert soups
salads
entrées
fruits
desserts

caroline barty

LAUREL
GLEN

San Diego, California

Published in the United States by

Laurel Glen Publishing

An imprint of the Advantage Publishers Group

5880 Oberlin Drive, San Diego, CA 92121-4794

www.advantagebooksonline.com

Copyright © MQ Publications Limited 2001

Text © Caroline Barty 2001

Project Editor: Nicola Birtwisle

Text Editor: Coralie Dorman

Designer: Elizabeth Ayer

Photography: Janine Hosegood

Stylist: Vanessa Kellas

Kitchen equipment kindly supplied by

Gill Wing Cookshop, London, England

Copyright under International, Pan American and Universal Copyright Conventions. All rights reserved. No part of this book may be reproduced in any form or by any means, electronic or mechanical, including photocopying, recording, or by any information storage and retrieval system, without written permission from the copyright holder. Brief passages (not to exceed 1,000 words) may be quoted for reviews.

All notations of errors or omissions should be addressed to Laurel Glen Publishing, editorial department, at the above address. All other correspondence (author inquiries, permissions and rights) concerning the content of this book should be addressed to MQ Publications, 12 The Ivories, 6–8 Northampton Street, London, England N1 2HY.

ISBN 1-57145-586-8

Library of Congress Cataloging-in-Publication Data available on request.

1 2 3 4 04 03 02 01

Printed and bound in England by Butler & Tanner Ltd

NOTE

Recipes using uncooked meat should be avoided by infants, the elderly, pregnant women, and anyone with a compromised immune system.

contents

introduction

From the moment you venture into the kitchen, it's a safe bet you are going to reach for at least one knife as you start to cook. This book is designed to help you choose the right knife for the right job and to make preparing food much easier—and enjoyable. Boning a chicken or leg of lamb can be a bit of a daunting prospect at the best of times, but use the correct knife and it'll make it a pleasurable achievement. Likewise, a small, blunt knife will drive you mad if you're trying to chop herbs, whereas it's a breeze with a sharp, large-bladed knife or mezzaluna. Similarly, complicated gourmet recipes are a snap when proper chopping technique is mastered.

If you are considering buying new knives—and they really are worth the investment—before you part with your cash, literally pick the knives up to see how comfortable they feel in your hand. Remember, looks alone aren't necessarily everything, but usually the more you pay the better the knife—and its looks. A good rule of thumb is that if the blade extends all the way into the handle, it means that its weight is evenly distributed and that the knife will last for years. Carbon steel knives have the sharpest edges, which are easily maintained. However, they discolor and rust easily so they need to be kept scrupulously clean and dry. High-carbon stainless steel knives are easy to sharpen, keep their edges longer, and they don't discolor.

Once you have invested in your knives, it makes sense to care for them. Keeping them in drawers might be convenient, but it's all too easy to cut yourself as you reach in, and knives can easily fall off magnetic strips. The best solution is to invest in a knife block, which will protect you and your knives.

A blunt knife is a dangerous knife, so always keep them razor-sharp. A large, heavy steel with a guard at the hilt is the best way of keeping knives sharp, but if you're not confident in your knife-sharpening skills then most good cookware stores will provide this service.

There are many recipes in this book which recommend the use of a food processor, but do try the more hands-on approach with a knife or other recommended hand instrument first. This will make you feel more in control of the texture and finished look of the dishes you are preparing, which is an important part of the food preparation learning curve. Once you are confident with manual techniques, then by all means use the processor.

In the instructions for some of the recipes, often a specific type of knife has been recommended to give the best results. Where no type is specified, just use the knife you feel most comfortable with—a chef's knife is ideal for everyday chopping and slicing.

equipment

The secret of good chopping is good equipment. Here is a selection of chopping boards, knives, and more specialized items. Start with the basics and expand your collection as you gain more expertise.

wooden chopping boards

A big, solid wooden chopping board is your kitchen's best friend. They don't look this perfect for long, but instead take on a comfortable, "distressed" look that will fill you with happy memories of all the meals you've cooked every time you look at it. Make sure you keep your board scrupulously clean, washing thoroughly with detergent between ingredients to avoid cross-contamination. Buy the best board you can afford and it'll last for years.

colored chopping boards To keep your kitchen hygienic, it's smart to have color-coded chopping boards. Keep green for chopping vegetables, pink for raw meat, blue for fish, and the others for cooked foods.

plastic chopping board Plastic chopping boards are cheaper and easier to keep clean, but don't last as long as the wooden variety.

mezzaluna with curved chopping board The "half moon" implement makes chopping herbs a breeze. Simply rock the blade to and fro across the special curved chopping board.

small paring knife
A handy knife to have around, this little wonder is great for peeling and slicing all your favorite vegetables.

serrated fruit knife Soft fruit and tomatoes demand a serrated knife. This one slices perfectly.

meat boning knife This knife has a curved blade and a sharp end which can tunnel through meat easily. Not suitable for any other job.

5-inch chef's knife Two basic chef's knives in different sizes should be an essential part of your kitchen kit.

8-inch chef's knife Chef's knives should be comfortably heavy, with large blades that are slightly curved from tip to heel.

steel The most effective way to sharpen knives. Select one that is good and heavy with a safety guard at the hilt

poultry shears These heavy-duty scissors, which have one serrated blade, can even cut through bone and cartilage.

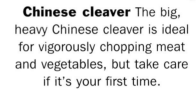

filleting knife This is the only knife to use when you've a fish to fillet. Its long, flexible blade is perfectly equipped to separate delicate flesh from spindly bones.

Chinese cleaver The big, heavy Chinese cleaver is ideal for vigorously chopping meat and vegetables, but take care if it's your first time.

Japanese cleaver These are similar to Chinese cleavers but are usually more expensive due to finer craftsmanship.

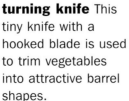

turning knife This tiny knife with a hooked blade is used to trim vegetables into attractive barrel shapes.

kitchen scissors Buy a sturdy, good quality pair of scissors with sharp blades. Scissors can handle any number of jobs around the kitchen, from snipping herbs straight from the plant to chopping bacon into a skillet.

food processor There are many models available, but it makes sense to buy a powerful one that has a wide range of chopping and slicing functions. This one even incorporates a blender.

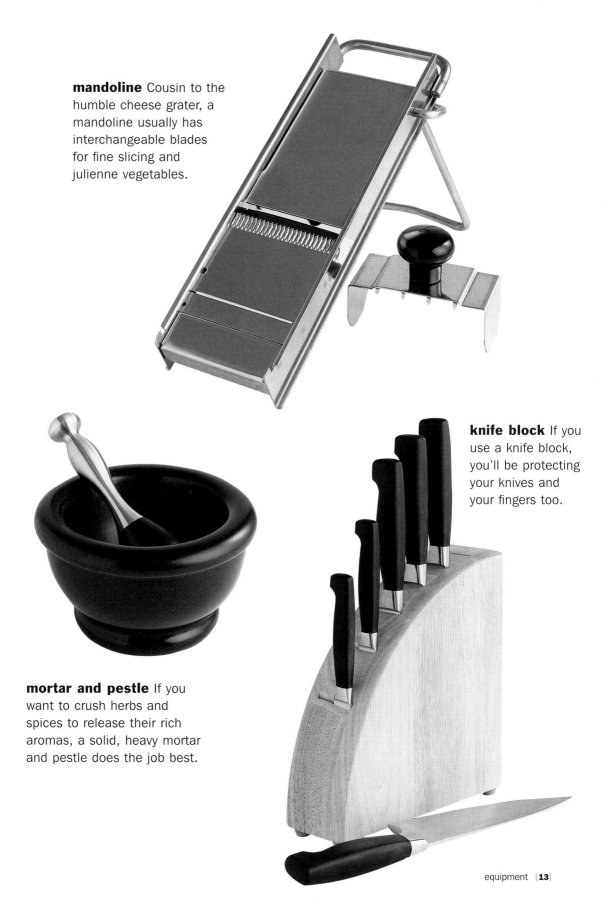

mandoline Cousin to the humble cheese grater, a mandoline usually has interchangeable blades for fine slicing and julienne vegetables.

knife block If you use a knife block, you'll be protecting your knives and your fingers too.

mortar and pestle If you want to crush herbs and spices to release their rich aromas, a solid, heavy mortar and pestle does the job best.

vegetables

vegetables introduction

There is something very soothing, even contemplative about chopping vegetables— the colors of the different piles of diced onions, carrots, and celery on the chopping board waiting for the pot, the clean white slices of an eggplant or the curly mound of a few sliced leeks. Simple to do, and it might seem, in certain recipes, that the chopping or slicing method is so straightforward as to not be worthy of mention.

However, the way the ingredients are chopped does have a bearing on the finished dish. For instance if the vegetables in the Provençal ratatouille (see page 65) were chopped too finely the result would be a burnt offering of unidentifiable charred vegetables instead of the delicious dish of chunky roasted vegetables bound in a tomato sauce that it is supposed to be.

Most of the recipes in this chapter require the basic chef's knife as the techniques described include traditional cuts like julienne (¼ in. thick and 1 in. long) and the standard dice (¼ in. square). A fruit knife—often the cheapest knife out of a set—is well worth using where more deft slicing, peeling, and chopping is required, especially with tomatoes.

When different equipment is called for, it is merely a recommendation because it is the best tool for the task, although obviously a knife will do the job too. For instance, the Deep-fried potato chips (see page 44) are easy to slice into the required paper-thin slivers with the razor-sharp blade of a mandoline, and a mortar and pestle makes a paste of herbs, oil, and nuts more efficiently than a knife when you are making simple sauces like basil-based pesto.

There are very few recipes in this part of the book that require an enormous amount of preparation or lengthy cooking, which make many of them firm favorites for that light lunch or even a first course when time is tight.

chopping vegetables

You can be guided as to which knife to use by the size and shape of the vegetable you are about to prepare. A large, knobbly celeriac is best tackled with a medium-sized, nonserrated blade, whereas a tomato yields wonderfully to the pressure of a incisive fruit knife. Bunch your fingers together to hold the vegetable in place—and also act as a valuable guard against nicking them with the knife—while you slice away with the knife in the other hand. Here's a selection of some of the most popular vegetables and how to chop them.

Dicing peppers Cut off both ends of the pepper. Make a cut from one end to the other and open the pepper out into a long strip. Trim off the white pith, remove the seeds, and cut into strips. Hold the strips together and cut into dice.

Dicing cucumber Peel the skin off with a small, sharp knife or vegetable peeler and cut in half lengthways. Run a small sharp-ended teaspoon down the center to remove the seeds. Cut into long strips, then into dice.

Slicing tomatoes Use a fruit knife and sharpen it well before attempting to cut a tomato. Depending on the type of tomato and the recipe, remove the watery seeds and any tough flesh from the stalk end.

Chopping sun-dried tomatoes Their sticky nature responds well to a mezzaluna—the rocking motion helps keep the pieces separate. Or try a large chef's knife, held at the point and lifted up and down, back and forth by the handle.

Chopping garlic Put the unpeeled garlic cloves on a board and place the thickest part of a chef's knife on top. Smash down with your fist to break them, remove the papery skin, then chop, finely, rocking the knife back and forth.

Chopping scallions Trim off most of the green part of the scallion, and cut a small slice off the root end to remove it. Run the point of a sharp knife down its length several times, then finely chop across the shreds.

Chopping squash Cut off the peel with a small sharp knife or vegetable peeler. Cut in half and scoop out all the seeds and fiber in the center. Cut each half into wedges, then chop each wedge into pieces.

Chopping parsley Employ the two-handed method for chopping parsley finely—indeed for chopping any herb. Hold the knife by the handle and the tip and rock backward and forward. Or snip herbs directly into your cooking pot with scissors held blades-downward for safety.

Slicing eggplant Trim the ends, then cut into slices. Eggplants used to need salting to bring out the bitter juices but this has been cultivated out of newer varieties. If you do want to salt your eggplant, put it in a colander, sprinkle with salt, leave 10 minutes then rinse.

Gazpacho

2 red bell peppers, deseeded · 1 green bell pepper, deseeded · ½ cucumber, peeled ·
2 scallions · 2 garlic cloves · 2 oz. slightly stale ciabatta or rustic bread (about 2 slices) ·
5 cups fresh tomato juice · 2 tbsp. white wine or sherry vinegar · 3 tbsp. olive oil ·
6 ice cubes · basil leaves to garnish · toasted croutons (optional)

SERVES 4

This wonderful cold soup originates from the Spanish region of Andalusia. It is an ideal soup to serve on a hot summer's day.

1. Finely dice the red and green peppers. Place about two-thirds in a large mixing bowl and reserve the rest for garnish.

2. Scrape the seeds out of the cucumber and finely dice. Place two-thirds in the bowl with the peppers and reserve the rest for garnish.

3. Finely chop the scallions and garlic and add to the mixing bowl.

4. Roughly cube the bread with a serrated knife and place in the mixing bowl. Pour the tomato juice and vinegar over the ingredients and add the olive oil. Mix and season well.

5. Using a blender or food processor, purée the soup in batches until smooth. Pour back into the bowl, add the ice cubes, and chill, at least 1 hour. Stir in the reserved diced vegetables and top with basil and croutons if desired.

Spring vegetable soup

2 leeks • 2 stalks celery • 2 tbsp. sunflower oil • 12 asparagus tips • 8 new potatoes •
5 cups vegetable stock • 1 cup shelled fresh peas • 3 tbsp. chopped fresh mint •
2 cups baby spinach leaves

SERVES 4–6

A deliciously light vegetable soup using the best spring ingredients. If you want a richer soup use a good homemade chicken stock.

1. Chop the leeks and celery into ½-inch slices using a medium-sized chopping knife. Heat the oil in a saucepan, add the leeks and celery and fry gently, 10 minutes. Don't let the leeks brown too much or they'll taste bitter.

2. Roughly chop the asparagus and cut the potatoes into bite-sized pieces. Add these to the pan with the stock, bring to a boil, then turn the heat down and simmer, 15 minutes. Add the peas and simmer an additional 5 minutes. Taste and season.

3. Stir the mint into the soup with the baby spinach leaves, then serve.

Cream of butternut squash and coconut soup

2 lbs. butternut squash • 1 onion • 1 red chili, deseeded • 2 tbsp. sunflower oil • 4 cups chicken broth or vegetable stock • 2 cups coconut milk • small bunch cilantro

SERVES 4

This soup has the most wonderful velvety texture and is extremely rich and filling. You can experiment with different kinds of squash depending on personal preference and market availability.

1. Peel the squash and cut in half with a large chopping knife. Scoop out the seeds and roughly chop the flesh. Roughly chop the onion and chili. Heat the oil in a fairly large saucepan and add the squash, onion, and chili. Cook, stirring, until the onion softens, 5–10 minutes.

2. Pour in the stock and simmer until the vegetables are tender, 20 minutes. Stir in the coconut milk. Let cool slightly then purée in a blender or food processor. Finely chop the cilantro and stir in just before serving.

Ribollita

3 stalks celery • 4 medium-sized carrots, peeled • 2 red onions • 5 tbsp. olive oil • 3 garlic cloves, finely chopped • 1 7-oz. can chopped tomatoes • 5 cups vegetable stock • 2 large handfuls cavolo nero, cabbage, or Swiss chard • 10-oz. can cooked borlotti or cannellini beans • small ciabatta loaf, about 6 oz.

SERVES 4–6

More of a vegetable stew than a soup, this is a hearty Italian dish, perfect for lunch on a cold winter's day. Cavolo nero is the authentic vegetable to use, but cabbage or Swiss chard are acceptable substitutes.

1. Using a medium-sized chef's knife, roughly chop the celery, carrots, and onions into bite-sized pieces. Heat the oil in a large saucepan. Add the vegetables and garlic and fry gently, 25–30 minutes. Stir every now and again to prevent the vegetables from burning.

2. Add the tomatoes and stock and simmer, 15 minutes. Roughly chop the cavolo nero and add to the pan with half the beans. Season well and simmer, an additional 20 minutes.

3. Mash or purée the remaining beans. Cut the bread into small cubes with a serrated bread knife. Stir both the beans and the bread into the soup and add a splash of extra-virgin olive oil just before serving.

Greek salad

4 tomatoes • ½ cucumber • ½ red onion • 2 tbsp. chopped fresh dill • 4 oz. feta cheese • ½ cup pitted black olives • 2 tbsp. olive oil • 1 tbsp. fresh lemon juice

SERVES 4–6

Dill is an unusual addition to this classic salad, but it marries surprisingly well with the tomatoes.

1. Roughly chop the tomatoes and cucumber and mix together in a salad bowl. Finely slice the onion and add to the salad along with the dill. Mix well and season with pepper. Feta cheese can be very salty so leave it up to the individual to add salt according to their own taste.

2. Cut the feta into small cubes and scatter over the salad with the olives. Whisk the olive oil with the lemon juice and pour over.

Panzanella (Italian bread salad)

1 small ciabatta or rustic loaf, about 6 oz. • 1 cucumber, peeled • 4 ripe tomatoes •
2 tbsp. capers • 2 garlic cloves • 2 tbsp. red wine vinegar • 8 tbsp. olive oil • 2 hard-
boiled eggs • 8–10 basil leaves

SERVES 6–8

**Choose the juiciest, ripest tomatoes for this traditional
Italian salad. Authentic versions call for chopped onion,
but the garlic-infused dressing in this version gives the
dish enough kick.**

1. Preheat the oven to 400° F. Cut the ciabatta into cubes with a
serrated bread knife. Toast in the oven, 10 minutes. Pour into a
high-sided salad bowl.

2. Halve the cucumber lengthwise and scrape out the seeds with a
spoon. Roughly chop with a medium-sized chopping knife and pile
onto the bread.

3. Peel the tomatoes, halve, and deseed. Cut into chunks and add
to the salad bowl. Sprinkle with capers.

To make the dressing, pound the garlic cloves in a mortar and
pestle. Whisk in the vinegar and oil and season. Pour over the
salad. Roughly chop the eggs and arrange on top of the salad with
the basil leaves. Leave 15 minutes then stir once before serving.
You want the bread to have soaked up the juices and dressing but
not to have become unappealingly soggy.

Raw fennel salad with Parmesan shavings

2 bulbs fennel • 1 tsp. grated lemon peel • 1 tbsp. fresh lemon juice •
4 tbsp. olive oil • 2-inch square piece Parmesan

SERVES 4

**This salad is simplicity itself and all the better for it.
Look for fat fennel bulbs rather than the long thin ones
as they have much more flavor.**

1. Fix the plain blade on a mandoline and finely slice the fennel.
Place in a large mixing bowl.

2. Mix the lemon peel and juice with the oil and season. Pour the
dressing over the fennel and leave 1 hour.

3. Shave the Parmesan on the same mandoline blade and scatter
the fennel on top just before serving.

Red pesto and ricotta stacks with eggplant and tomato

1 large eggplant • 2 tbsp. olive oil • 2 beefsteak tomatoes
For the red pesto • 2 red bell peppers • 2 garlic cloves • ⅓ cup pine nuts • ½ cup basil • 1- x 2-inch
piece Parmesan • 2 tbsp. ricotta • 2 tbsp. olive oil

SERVES 6 as a starter

A gutsy starter to serve with a plain green salad and charbroiled ciabatta slices.

1. Preheat the oven to 400° F. Halve and deseed the peppers. Put on a baking tray cut side down and place under a hot broiler until the skins are charred, 10–15 minutes. Put the peppers in a plastic bag until cool. Peel off the skins.

2. Place in a food processor with the remaining pesto ingredients and blend to a rough paste.

3. Cut the eggplant into 1-inch thick slices. Heat the oil in a skillet and brown the eggplant, 2 minutes each side. Drain on paper towels. You will probably need to do this in batches, in which case use a touch more oil.

4. Thickly slice the tomatoes. Lay four of the largest eggplant slices on a nonstick baking tray. Spread a heaped teaspoon of the pesto over each slice and top with a slice of tomato. Continue this once more ending with a slice of tomato.

5. Cook in the oven, 15 minutes. Be careful as you transfer them to serving plates.

Using a food processor to blend everything together for the pesto sauce does a quick and thorough job, but if you've time, why not try it by hand, in a large mortar and pestle?

Roasted red pepper and corn salsa

3 red bell peppers • 3 medium ears of corn • 4 tbsp. olive oil • 1 red chili • 1 garlic clove • 4 tbsp. lime juice

SERVES 3–4 as an accompaniment

This fresh zingy salsa is a great partner for charbroiled chicken or barbecued lamb.

1. Halve the peppers through the stalks and deseed. Place cut side down on a baking tray and cook under a hot broiler until the skins char and the flesh has softened, about 15 minutes. Put in a plastic bag and allow to cool. Peel off the skins.

2. With a large knife scrape the kernels off the ears of corn. Heat 1 tbsp. oil in a saucepan and fry the kernels, 5 minutes. Transfer to a mixing bowl.

3. Finely dice the roasted pepper halves. Cut the chili in half, deseed, and finely dice. Stir the pepper and chili into the corn. Mince the garlic and mix into the salsa with the lime juice and remaining oil.

Radicchio salad with crispy bacon

2 heads radicchio • 6 slices bacon • 3 tbsp. olive oil • 1 tbsp. balsamic vinegar • 1 tsp. French grain mustard

SERVES 4

Sometimes the best flavor combinations are the simplest. Make this one at the last minute to retain its freshness.

1. Peel the outer leaves of the radicchio and halve lengthwise through the root. Cut out the hard core. Place cut side down on a board and finely slice. Arrange in a shallow salad bowl.

2. Finely dice the bacon. Heat the olive oil in a skillet and slowly fry the bacon until crispy, 10 minutes.

3. Stir in the vinegar and mustard and heat through. Pour over the radicchio and serve immediately.

Roasted beet salad with oranges and goat cheese

6 medium-sized fresh beets, washed • 1 tbsp. balsamic vinegar • 1 tsp. honey • 4 tbsp. olive oil • 2 oranges • 5 oz. goat cheese • 1 tbsp. chopped fresh chives

SERVES 4

Use fresh beets to bring out the full flavor of this salad—although canned, precooked beets can be used as a substitute. Use whichever kind of goat cheese you like best— mature French chèvre is a good one.

1. Preheat the oven to 350° F. Pierce the beets with a skewer or point of a sharp knife and place in a roasting pan. Roast until tender, 1½ hours. Cool then peel off the skins. Cut into ½-inch thick slices and put into a serving bowl.

2. Mix the vinegar, honey, and oil together and pour over the beets.

3. With a serrated fruit knife, peel the oranges and cut into segments (see page 140). Add to the beets and crumble the goat cheese on top. Scatter with chives before serving.

Dill and cucumber salad

1 cucumber, peeled · 1 small bunch fresh dill · 1 tbsp. red wine vinegar · 2 tsp. sugar · 2 tbsp. sunflower oil

SERVES 4

This is another incredibly easy but delicious salad, great served with a plate of smoked salmon.

1. Finely slice the cucumber on the plain blade of a mandoline and arrange on a flat plate.

2. Finely chop the dill with a medium-sized chopping knife and sprinkle over the cucumber. Stir the sugar into the vinegar until it dissolves and whisk in the oil. Pour over the cucumber and season with fine sea salt and pepper.

The mandoline is the perfect tool for cutting wafer-thin slices of cucumber.

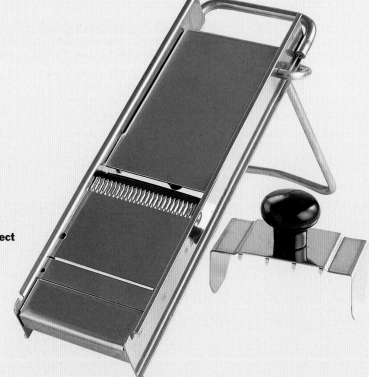

Spiced eggplant salad

1 onion • 2 garlic cloves • 5 tbsp. olive oil • 2 small eggplant • 2 tsp. ground cumin • 1 tsp. ground cinnamon • 2 tomatoes, skinned • ⅓ cup raisins • small bunch cilantro

SERVES 4

This salad, *imam bayeldi*, has its origins in the Middle East where it was supposed to have made the sultans faint with delight. True or not, this is a deliciously fragrant salad that can be served warm or chilled.

1. Finely chop the onion and garlic with a medium-sized chopping knife. Heat 2 tbsp. oil in a wok and fry until soft and golden, 15 minutes.

2. Cut the eggplant into small cubes, about ½-inch square. Add to the wok with the remaining oil and fry, 10 minutes. Stir in the spices and cook, 2–3 minutes.

3. Finely chop the tomatoes and stir into the eggplant mixture with the raisins. Season and cook an additional 5 minutes. Finely chop the cilantro and carefully stir into the salad.

Patatas bravas

5 medium-sized potatoes, peeled • 6 tbsp. olive oil • 1 red onion, chopped • 3 garlic cloves, chopped • 1 tbsp. paprika • pinch or more chili flakes • 14-oz. can chopped tomatoes • 1 tbsp. chopped fresh oregano

SERVES 4

These "fierce potatoes" are a regular feature on any Spanish tapas menu. Serve them as part of a tapas menu or as an accompaniment to broiled steak or chicken.

1. Chop the potatoes into rough 1½-inch cubes. Parboil in salted boiling water, 5 minutes, then drain well.

2. Heat 4 tbsp. oil in a large skillet, add the potatoes and fry slowly, 15 minutes. Transfer the potatoes to an ovenproof serving dish and keep warm in a moderate oven.

3. Heat the remaining oil in the skillet and fry the onion and garlic until golden, 10 minutes. Add the paprika and chili flakes and fry an additional 2 minutes. Drain most of the excess juice from the tomatoes then add to the fried onion mixture. Cook 5 minutes, stir in the oregano and pour the sauce over the potatoes.

New York potato salad

18 new potatoes • 3 stalks celery • 4 scallions • 1 small bunch parsley • 1 small bunch chives • ½ cup sour cream • ¾ cup mayonnaise • 1 tbsp. fresh lemon juice • 2 hard-boiled eggs

SERVES 6

For a good potato salad you need to pick the potato variety carefully. A floury potato will result in a lumpy mash of a salad, so find good waxy new potatoes like Long Whites. The same goes for the mayonnaise. If it's homemade, all the better, but a superior store-bought brand will do.

1. Cook the potatoes in boiling salted water until tender, 15–20 minutes. Let cool a while then peel off the skins. This is a bit tedious but worth the effort. Chop into bite-sized pieces with a medium chopping knife and transfer to a mixing bowl.

2. Finely chop the celery, scallions, and parsley and mix into the potatoes. Snip the chives into little pieces with kitchen scissors and add to the rest of the ingredients.

3. Whisk the sour cream, mayonnaise, and lemon juice together, add plenty of black pepper and pour over the salad. Mix everything well. Roughly chop the eggs and carefully fold into the potato salad. Chill until ready to serve.

Coleslaw

1 medium-sized white cabbage • 2 carrots, peeled • 1 stick celery • 1 apple, cored • ⅓ cup raisins • small bunch chives • ½ cup mayonnaise • 1 cup plain yogurt • 1 tsp. white wine vinegar

SERVES 8–10

Coleslaw is everybody's favorite, and if you've never made your own, you will be surprised at the creamy subtlety of flavors compared to supermarket brands which tend to be soggy and acidic.

1. Slice the cabbage and carrots on the fine julienne blade of a mandoline and mix together in a large bowl.

2. Finely chop the celery and apple. Add to the cabbage along with the raisins and stir well.

3. Snip the chives with a pair of scissors and mix into the coleslaw. Whisk the mayonnaise, yogurt, and vinegar together and season. Pour the dressing over the coleslaw and toss together. Chill until ready to serve.

Old-fashioned English chips with tomato and anchovy mayonnaise

6 medium-sized russet potatoes, peeled • oil for deep frying • 1 whole egg •
2 egg yolks • 2 tsp. English mustard powder • 1 tbsp. white wine vinegar •
1¼ cups light olive oil or peanut oil • 5 anchovy fillets • 3 pieces sun-dried tomatoes •
1 tbsp. fresh lemon juice (optional)

SERVES 4

Take a tip from the English: there really is nothing better than a plate of homemade chips—french fries—with a tangy mayonnaise for dipping.

1. Peel the potatoes, cut into chips and drop into a bowl of cold water. Set aside while the oil heats up.

2. Heat the oil for deep frying in a deep fat fryer to 325° F. Drain the potatoes well and pat dry on paper towels. Fry in batches until soft and pale, 6–8 minutes each batch, transferring to a plate lined with paper towels.

3. Increase the temperature of the oil to 375° F. Re-fry the chips, in batches, until crisp and golden, 3–4 minutes each batch. Drain on paper towels and keep warm.

4. For the mayonnaise, put the egg and egg yolks in a food processor with the mustard and vinegar and blend for a few seconds. With the motor running, slowly pour in the oil. When the mixture has emulsified and thickened add the anchovies and sun-dried tomatoes and blend until smooth. If it is very thick, blend in the lemon juice.

Peel the potatoes with a small knife or a vegetable peeler, then using a large chef's knife, cut off the rounded edges to make the potatoes into even rectangles.

Cut each potato rectangle into ½-inch-wide strips, then again lengthways into chips. Fill a bowl with cold water and drop in the chips as they are made. This removes the starch.

Straw potato cake

4 medium-sized potatoes, peeled • 1 onion • 2 tbsp. olive oil • ¼ cup shredded cheddar

SERVES 4

1. Slice the potatoes into matchsticks with the thin julienne blade on a mandoline. Put in a bowl and season. Finely slice the onion with a medium-sized chopping knife.

2. Heat the oil in a small nonstick skillet and fry the onion until soft and golden, 10 minutes. Add the potatoes to the skillet and pat down to form a cake. Fry gently, 15 minutes.

3. Lay a large plate over the skillet and tip it upside down so the cake is on the plate. Slide it back into the skillet and continue to fry, 15 minutes.

4. Sprinkle the cheese over the top and put under a hot broiler for 3–4 minutes until bubbling. Serve immediately.

Serve this cheesy little wonder with sausages for a hearty brunch.

Deep-fried potato chips

3 potatoes, peeled • oil for deep-frying • sea salt

SERVES 4 as a snack

1. Slice the potatoes on the thin plain blade of a mandoline. Place in a bowl of cold water and rinse well. Drain and pat dry.

2. Heat the oil to 350° F in a deep fryer. Fry the potatoes until crisp and golden, 4–5 minutes. Drain on paper towels and sprinkle with sea salt.

You will never want to go back to store-bought chips after these. If you want a change, fry a mixture of plain and sweet potatoes.

Spicy tomato and apple chutney

14 tomatoes, skinned · 5 large onions · 6 tart apples, peeled and cored · 2 garlic cloves · 1½ cups raisins · 2 tbsp. English mustard powder · 1 tbsp. paprika · 1 tbsp. ground coriander · 4 tsp. salt · 2 tsp. curry powder · 3½ cups malt vinegar · scant 2 cups sugar

MAKES about 5 lbs.

Homemade chutneys are really worth the time spent on them and are infinitely more delicious than the store-bought variety. Perfect for using up leftover fruits and vegetables from harvest time in your garden.

1. Chop the tomatoes, onions, and apples into large or small chunks, whichever you prefer. Finely chop the garlic.

2. Place all the ingredients in a preserving pan and stir well. Bring to a boil, reduce the heat to low, and simmer, stirring occasionally until all the liquid has evaporated, 3 hours.

3. Spoon into sterilized jars, cover, and seal. Leave in a cool, dry place for at least 3 months for the flavors to mature.

Risotto primavera

1 onion • 1 stick celery • 2 carrots, peeled • 2 tbsp. butter • 1 tbsp. olive oil • 1¾ cups arborio rice • 4 cups chicken broth • ½ cup fresh peas • 2 medium zucchini • small bunch mint • small bunch parsley • Parmesan for serving

SERVES 6

To make the perfect risotto, you don't have to stand over it stirring like crazy—stirring every now and then when you add the stock gives great results.

1. Finely chop the onion, celery, and carrots. Melt the butter with the oil in a large heavy-based saucepan and add the vegetables. Cover and cook, 15 minutes.

2. Add the rice to the pan and stir well to coat the grains of rice. Pour in about ½ cup broth and stir. Cook until the liquid has been absorbed.

3. Add the same amount of broth and the peas, stir a few times and again leave to let the rice absorb the liquid. Continue in this way leaving ½ cup broth in reserve, about 25 minutes.

4. Finely chop the zucchini and stir into the risotto with the remaining broth. Stir well and season.

5. Finely chop the mint and parsley with a mezzaluna and mix into the risotto. This dish does not like to hang around so serve immediately with shavings of Parmesan.

Fettuccine with tomato and basil sauce

6 plum tomatoes • 1 small bunch basil • 3 garlic cloves • 4 tbsp. olive oil •
1 lb. fettuccine • Parmesan to serve

SERVES 4

This is simple but spectacular—like all the best pasta sauces. Less is more.

1. Peel, halve, and deseed the tomatoes then roughly chop and spoon into a mixing bowl. Roughly chop the basil and garlic and place in a mortar and pestle with the oil. Pound until smooth.

2. Season the tomatoes and stir into the basil and garlic sauce.

3. Cook the pasta until al dente, 10–12 minutes, then drain, reserving 1 tbsp. of the cooking liquor. Return the fettuccine to the pan and stir in the tomato and basil sauce and the liquor. Serve immediately with Parmesan.

Stuffed mushrooms with Gruyère cheese and bacon

4 slices bacon • 3 leeks • 2 tbsp. butter • 1 tbsp. olive oil • 3-inch square
piece Gruyère cheese • 1½ cups fresh white bread crumbs • 1 small bunch
tarragon • 8 large portobello mushrooms

SERVES 4 as a main course, 8 as a starter

These mushrooms are wonderfully tasty, oozing with a melted cheese, bacon, and leek stuffing. Serve simply with crusty bread to sop up the juices.

1. For the stuffing, finely dice the bacon and finely slice the leeks. Melt the butter with the oil in a skillet and fry the bacon and leeks, 10 minutes. Transfer to a mixing bowl and let cool a little. Preheat the oven to 375° F.

2. Finely dice the cheese and stir into the leek and bacon mixture along with the bread crumbs. Finely chop the tarragon with a mezzaluna before adding to the stuffing.

3. Clean and peel the mushrooms and cut off the stumpy stalks. Put the mushrooms flat side down in a very well oiled roasting pan. Season then pile the stuffing mixture into the mushroom cavities. Cook in the oven until browned and bubbling, 20–25 minutes.

chopping an onion

Everyone has their own way of chopping an onion—and everyone swears that their method is the best, the only one that will work. This quick and easy method guarantees a tear-free experience and neatly chopped onion.

The secret lies in the root end. In here is the substance that makes the eyes stream, but although its devilish in that way, it has a second role to play, that of a handle and lynchpin that holds the whole onion together without it falling apart as you chop. And, as you never cut into it, apart from to cut it in half, you'll find there are no tears. First of all, cut the onion in half through the root end and tip, using a large chef's knife. Use the blade to ease the brown papery skin off, then cut the tip end off both halves, leaving the root ends intact.

step 1 Make sure you leave the root end intact. Take the point of the knife and make incisions, starting just slightly away from the root end, down to the tip end.

step 2 Make several cuts across the onion half, again not quite reaching the root end. Two or three cuts should be enough, but it depends on how finely the onion needs to be chopped.

step 3 Using the uncut root end as a sort of handle, cut across each onion half to make onion dice. When you reach the root end and can cut no more, simply throw the root away.

Braised lamb shanks with mirepoix vegetables

2 carrots, peeled • 3 stalks celery • 1 large onion • 2 garlic cloves • 1 tbsp. olive oil • 4 lamb shanks • scant 2 cups red wine • 1 cup lamb stock or chicken broth • 1 tbsp. tomato paste • 2 bay leaves • 2 sprigs rosemary

SERVES 4

Lamb shanks should be cooked until the meat is nearly falling off the bone. This gives the casserole an incredible intensity. This trio of vegetables—carrots, celery, and onion—are an essential base for many European dishes and here they are finely diced to become part of the sauce. Serve with creamy mashed potatoes.

1. Preheat the oven to 300° F. Cut the carrots and celery into very fine strips and finely dice. Finely chop the onion and garlic.

2. Heat the oil in a large casserole and brown the lamb shanks all over, about 10 minutes. Transfer to a plate.

3. Fry the vegetables until they start to take on a little color, 15 minutes. Return the lamb shanks to the casserole and pour the wine and stock over them. Add the tomato paste, bay leaves, and rosemary, and season well.

4. Bring to a boil, cover with a lid, and cook in the oven, 3–3½ hours. Turn the meat occasionally during cooking.

Roasted vegetables with pine nuts and Parmesan

8 small new potatoes · 4 small parsnips, peeled · 4 tbsp. olive oil · 6 baby leeks ·
4 asparagus spears · 2 tbsp. pine nuts, toasted · ¼ cup Parmesan · ¼ cup fresh white
bread crumbs

SERVES 4

**Roasted vegetables take on a wonderful intensity of
flavor. The nut and cheese crumb topping finishes off the
dish perfectly.**

1. Preheat the oven to 400° F. Cut the potatoes in half. If the
parsnips are large cut into quarters lengthwise, but if they're small
simply halve them. Pour the oil into a roasting pan, add the
vegetables, and toss well to coat in the oil. Season and roast in
oven for 30 minutes.

2. Trim the leeks and asparagus and add to the roasting pan. Toss
all the vegetables together and roast an additional 25 minutes.

3. Coarsely grate the Parmesan and put in a food processor with
the pine nuts and bread crumbs. Blend for a couple of seconds until
the nuts have just broken up.

4. Sprinkle the mixture over the roasted vegetables and return to
the oven until crispy and golden, 5 more minutes.

Pesto and tomato tarts

2 small bunches basil • 2 garlic cloves • ⅓ cup pine nuts • 3- x 1-inch piece Parmesan • 6 tbsp. olive oil • 13 oz. puff pastry • 4 tomatoes • 6 sun-dried tomatoes

SERVES 4

A tasty starter or light lunch. This recipe makes a larger quantity of pesto than you will need but it keeps for 3–4 weeks in a fridge so use it on pasta or pizzas or stirred into stews at a later date.

1. Preheat the oven to 425° F. Roughly chop the basil and garlic and place in a large mortar and pestle with the pine nuts. Roughly grate the Parmesan and add to the basil and garlic. Pour in 2 tbsp. of the oil and pound to a paste, slowly adding the remaining oil.

2. Roll out the pastry to a 12-inch square. Cut out four 6-inch rounds and put on a baking tray. Spread 1 tbsp. of pesto onto each round.

3. Thinly slice the tomatoes and arrange on top of the pesto. Finely chop the sun-dried tomatoes and scatter over the tomatoes.

4. Bake until the pastry is puffed and golden, 15–20 minutes.

Turned carrots with maple syrup

8 carrots, peeled · small bunch parsley · 2 tbsp. butter · 2 tbsp. maple syrup

SERVES 4

Turning vegetables—whittling them into uniform barrel shapes—takes a special knife and a bit of practice but looks very sophisticated on the dinner table.

1. Top and tail the carrots and cut into even-sized pieces, about 2 inches long. Using a little turning knife trim the carrots into barrel shaped pieces. Reserve the discarded carrot trimmings to use in stocks and soups at a later date. Finely chop the parsley.

2. Melt the butter in a large saucepan and pour in about ½ cup water. You need roughly ½ inch in the bottom of the pan. Add the carrots and stir well to coat them in liquid. Cover and simmer, 12–15 minutes.

3. Remove the lid, turn the heat up, and bubble to reduce the liquid to about 2 tbsp. Add the maple syrup, stir and bubble 1 minute.

4. Stir in the chopped parsley and serve immediately.

Parsley and leek frittata

3 leeks · 2 tbsp. butter · 2 small bunches parsley · 4 large eggs

SERVES 4

The Italian version of the omelet, this requires no cooking skills whatsoever. It makes a wonderful, light lunch with a green salad or wrapped up and served as part of a picnic.

1. Finely slice the leeks on the diagonal. Melt the butter in a medium-sized skillet and add the leeks. Cook until soft, 8–10 minutes.

2. Remove the stalks from the parsley and finely chop with a mezzaluna. Stir into leeks.

3. Beat the eggs and season. Pour into the skillet and cook gently, about 10 minutes. The base of the frittata should be set, but the top will be wobbly.

4. Place the skillet under a preheated broiler and broil until the top is set and golden, 3–4 minutes.

Roquefort and arugula custards

2 large handfuls arugula • 1 ¼ cups half-and-half • 5-inch square piece Roquefort •
1 whole egg • 3 egg yolks

SERVES 4 as a starter or light lunch

**The subtle peppery flavor of the wilted arugula marries
well with the salty piquancy of Roquefort, that most
excellent of French blue cheeses. Serve the custards in
the ramekins or turn out onto the serving dishes and
garnish with fresh arugula leaves.**

1. Preheat the oven to 300° F. Stuff the arugula into a saucepan,
cover, and cook for 1–2 minutes until wilted. Let cool then squeeze
out any liquid.

2. Put the cooked arugula in a food processor with the cream and
the Roquefort. Season then blend until smooth. Add the whole egg
and egg yolks and blend briefly to mix.

3. Pour the mixture into four well-buttered 4-oz. ramekins. Place in
a bain-marie in the oven and cook until just set, 35–40 minutes.
Remove from the oven and leave 5 minutes before serving.

Goat cheese and zucchini mousse

10 oz. fresh goat cheese • 3 oz. chèvre or mature goat cheese • 3 tbsp. sour cream • 2 large eggs • small bunch tarragon • 2 medium-sized zucchini • 1 tbsp. butter

SERVES 4 as a starter or light lunch

These pretty little mousses are easy to make and very delicious. Serve as a first course.

1. Preheat the oven to 375° F. Place both goat cheeses, sour cream, eggs, and tarragon in a food processor. Season and blend until smooth.

2. Top and tail the zucchini and with a vegetable peeler peel off strips lengthwise down the zucchini. Butter four 6-oz. dariole molds and line each with strips of zucchini. Trim the ends if they protrude over the tops of the molds.

3. Spoon the cheese mixture into the molds and place on a baking tray.

4. Cook in the oven until firm, 20 minutes. Allow to rest for a couple of minutes then unmold onto serving plates.

Falafels with herb and yogurt dip

For the falafels • 1-lb. can cooked chick peas • 2 garlic cloves • 1 tbsp. tahini paste •
2 tsp. ground cumin • 1 tsp. turmeric • ½ tsp. cayenne pepper • 2 eggs • 1 small
bunch cilantro • flour, seasoned with salt and pepper to taste • oil for deep frying
For the dip • 1 small bunch mint • 1 small bunch parsley • 1 small bunch chives • 1 cup
plain yogurt

SERVES 4

**Serve these Middle Eastern patties stuffed in pita breads
spread with the herb dip.**

1. Place all the ingredients for the falafel, except the flour and oil
for frying, in a food processor, season, and blend until smooth.

2. Shape the mixture into patties, about 1 tbsp. of mixture per
patty, and roll in the seasoned flour. Heat the oil to 350° F and
deep-fry the falafel patties until golden, 3–4 minutes. Drain on
paper towels.

3. Finely chop the herbs with a mezzaluna and mix with the yogurt.
Taste and season again if necessary. Serve the falafel warm with the
dip on the side.

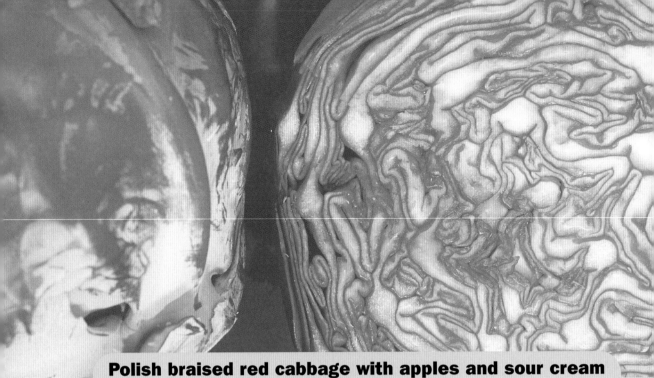

Polish braised red cabbage with apples and sour cream

1 red cabbage, approximately 2 lbs. • 2 dessert apples, peeled and cored •
6 tbsp. butter • ⅓ cup sugar • 4 tbsp. balsamic vinegar • ½ cup sour cream • 1 tbsp.
chopped parsley

SERVES 6–8

**A gutsy, warming winter dish, it is the perfect
accompaniment to roast pork. The flavors are even
better if you cook it a day in advance.**

1. Preheat the oven to 325° F. With a large chopping knife halve
the cabbage and finely slice. Using a smaller fruit knife cut the
apples into eight pieces.

2. Place half the chopped cabbage in a large Dutch oven then
cover with the apples. Dot with half the butter and sprinkle over half
the sugar. Season. Pile in the remaining cabbage, sprinkle with the
remaining butter and sugar, and pour in the vinegar. Cover and cook
in the oven, 1¾ hours. Halfway through cooking give the cabbage a
good stir to mix up the ingredients. Just before serving,, spoon the
sour cream over it and sprinkle with chopped parsley.

Provençal ratatouille

2 bulbs fennel • 3 red onions • 6 garlic cloves • 6 tbsp. olive oil • 3 zucchini •
2 red bell peppers, deseeded • 1 eggplant • 14-oz. can chopped tomatoes •
½ cup white wine • 2 tbsp. tomato paste • 6 sprigs fresh thyme • 1 tsp. sugar

SERVES 4

Classic ratatouille is a dish of roasted vegetables lightly covered in a rich sauce. Serve it hot or cold (especially good with barbecued meat), or for a complete vegetarian meal, top it with slices of smoked mozzarella and place under the broiler until golden.

1. Preheat the oven to 400° F. You will need two large roasting pans for this. Don't try to cram all the vegetables into one or they'll end up soggy and stewed instead of roasted. Cut the fennel into quarters lengthwise and blanch in boiling water, 5 minutes. Quarter the onions. Put the fennel and onions in a roasting pan with three unpeeled garlic cloves and half the oil. Season well and roast in the top of the oven, 50 minutes.

2. Cut the zucchini into ½-inch slices and chop the peppers into large chunks. Cut the eggplant into 2-inch chunks. Pour the remaining oil over the vegetables, add the rest of the garlic cloves and roast on the second shelf of the oven, 40 minutes.

3. Meanwhile make the tomato sauce. Empty the tomatoes into a saucepan and stir in the remaining ingredients. Simmer until reduced and thickened, 20 minutes. Remove the thyme sprigs and stir the roasted vegetables into the tomato sauce.

All seasons pizza

1 small trimmed head broccoli · 1 heaped cup button mushrooms · 1 garlic clove ·
2 tbsp. olive oil · 6-oz. can artichoke hearts · 2-inch piece pepperoni · 1 ball
mozzarella · 6 tbsp. tomato sauce · 8-inch ready-made pizza base

SERVES 1 or 2 depending on appetite

**There is nothing more satisfying than making your own
pizza. Use a ready-made pizza base or make your own.**

1. Preheat the oven to 425° F. Blanch the broccoli in salted boiling
water, 2 minutes. Drain well and roughly chop. Set aside.

2. Finely slice the mushrooms and garlic. Heat the olive oil in a
skillet and fry the mushrooms and garlic for 5 minutes.

3. Halve the artichoke hearts and thinly slice the pepperoni and
mozzarella.

4. Spread the tomato sauce over the pizza base. Arrange the
vegetables evenly over the pizza, dot with slices of pepperoni and
scatter over the mozzarella slices.

5. Drizzle with a touch of olive oil and bake in the oven, 15–20
minutes.

Thai green chicken curry

2-inch piece fresh ginger, peeled · 2 garlic cloves · 1 stick lemon grass · 4 scallions · 2 tbsp. sunflower oil · 1½ lbs. boneless chicken thighs · 2 tbsp. soy sauce · 1 tbsp. Thai fish sauce (nam pla) · 14-oz. can coconut milk · 2 kaffir lime leaves · 8 shiitake mushrooms · 1 small bunch fresh cilantro · 1 small bunch fresh basil

For the green Thai curry paste · 6 green chilis, deseeded · 2 Thai green chilis, deseeded · 5 garlic cloves · 2-inch piece fresh ginger, peeled · 4 scallions · 2 sticks lemon grass · 5 kaffir lime leaves · 8 cilantro stalks, washed · 1 small bunch cilantro

SERVES 4

Home-made curry paste is so much fresher than the store-bought kind. Any leftover paste will keep in the refrigerator for a few weeks. Serve with Thai sticky rice.

1. Roughly chop all the ingredients for the curry paste then transfer to a mortar and pestle and pound to a paste. Add a little water if the mixture becomes difficult to break down. Set aside.

2. Finely chop the ginger, garlic, and lemon grass. Finely slice the scallions. Cut the chicken into 2-inch pieces.

Using a mortar and pestle to pound the ingredients together really brings out their flavors to their best advantage.

3. Heat the oil in a wok and stir-fry the ginger, garlic, lemon grass, and scallions, 3–4 minutes. Add the chicken pieces and stir-fry an additional 3–4 minutes. Stir in 2 tbsp. of the curry paste, the soy sauce, and the fish sauce. Add the coconut milk and lime leaves, and simmer 10 minutes before adding the mushrooms. Simmer an additional 15 minutes.

4. Finely chop the cilantro and basil and stir into the curry just before serving.

meat & poultry

meat & poultry
introduction

There can be few more delicious things to eat than properly prepared and carefully cooked meat. Half the secret of good meat cooking is knowing which cut suits which method of cooking. The wonderful slow-cooked Spanish pork recipe (see page 82) would have none of the depth of flavor or richness if a piece of pork loin were used instead of a belly or shoulder cut.

It is always worth making friends with your local butcher, who will gladly undertake the tasks of boning or jointing, but it's still a skill worth learning. Plus, when you are done, you have the lamb bones and chicken carcasses to drop into a pot with a few vegetables, peppercorns, and herbs to make delicious homemade stock—and stock can transport a dish from the mundane to the sublime. Interestingly, a boning knife should never be too sharp, as it is required to tunnel and ease meat off a bone rather than slice through it.

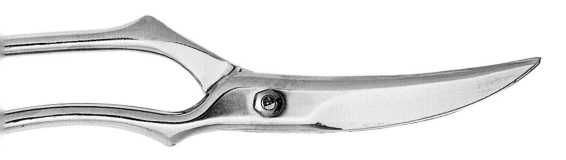

Because of its density and sometimes sinewy texture, cutting meat into cubes for a casserole or into slices requires the weightiest knife with the sharpest blade. Carpaccio of beef (see page 84) is the perfect example of this—there is no way you can prepare the wafer-thin slices without the right knife. Ultrasharp Chinese or Japanese cleavers are also great for chopping meat and once you have the feel of them, it's hard not to use them for everything.

A whole chicken can be chopped up using a large, heavy chef's knife or a cleaver, with specialized poultry shears or even a sturdy pair of kitchen scissors. Don't attempt this with a serrated knife as it will literally mash the flesh as you cut and tear the skin.

Every occasion is accounted for when you cook meat and poultry: dishes from the quickly pan-fried steak or chicken breast to long slow braises and roasts. And it's useful to know how to prepare it as the professionals do.

boning a leg of lamb

Do this when you have plenty of time to spare and take it slowly. This technique needs a little careful practice.

A boning knife is an essential piece of equipment if you want to bone out a leg or shoulder of lamb. Its specially designed shape and sharp, pointed end make for an effortless task—larger, less flexible knives simply won't be able to cope with the irregular angles that have to be dealt with. Of course a good butcher will do the job for you, but it's a useful skill to acquire.

step 1 Put the lamb on a board and, starting from the thick ball joint end, start tunneling through the leg with a boning knife, keeping the blade as close to the bone as possible.

step 2 This is fairly straightforward until you reach the next joint, which is where the shin bone meets the knee. Loosen the meat which is surrounding the joint.

step 3 Turn the meat around and start working on the ankle end. Use the boning knife in the same way to tunnel through to meet the at the joint.

step 4 By now the bone should be free. If it isn't, just keep working away with the boning knife until you can easily pull the whole bone out of the lamb.

Boned leg of lamb with acorn squash and rosemary

4 lbs. leg of lamb • 1 acorn squash • 3 tbsp. olive oil • 4 unpeeled garlic cloves • 1 red onion • 4 sprigs rosemary • ½ cup fresh white bread crumbs • 1 tbsp. pine nuts, toasted • 2 tbsp. butter

SERVES 4

A fabulous specialty roast which cuts out tricky carving. There's no bone so it'll slice like a dream.

1. Preheat the oven to 400° F. Put the lamb on a board and using a boning knife, take out the bone.

2. Pare or peel off the skin from the squash and remove the seeds. Cut into ½-inch pieces. Pour 2 tbsp. oil into a roasting pan, add the squash and garlic, and toss well to coat in the oil. Roast 35 minutes. The squash should be just soft. Transfer to a mixing bowl and cool.

3. Finely chop the onion and fry in the remaining oil 10 minutes. Mix with the squash and allow to cool. Finely chop the rosemary and mix into the onion and squash mixture, adding the bread crumbs and pine nuts. Taste and adjust the seasoning.

4. Using your hands, stuff the mixture into the leg cavity. Tie with five or six pieces of string to prevent the stuffing from falling out. Smear the leg with the butter and roast about 1½ hours, basting the meat every now and then. Allow the meat to rest 15 minutes before carving into slices.

Rack of lamb with cucumber, mint, and tarragon

1 medium-sized cucumber • 2 racks of lamb with 6 chops in each • 2 tbsp. butter •
1 tsp. white wine vinegar • 4 tbsp. white wine • 1¼ cups heavy cream • 1 small bunch
mint • 1 small bunch tarragon

SERVES 4

**Similar in texture to zucchini, cooked cucumber has a
more intriguing and underrated taste.**

1. Peel the cucumber, scrape out the seeds, and slice into boat-
shaped pieces. Put in a colander and sprinkle with a little salt. Set
aside until the juices run, 20 minutes. Rinse well under cold water
and pat dry. Preheat the oven to 400° F.

2. Season the racks of lamb and put in a roasting pan. Roast
25–30 minutes.

3. Melt the butter in a skillet and gently fry the cucumber until
softened, 10 minutes. Turn the heat up and add the vinegar and
white wine. Reduce until there is no liquid left in the pan. Turn the
heat down and stir in the cream. Simmer 5–6 minutes. Taste and
adjust the seasoning.

4. Finely chop the mint and tarragon and just before serving stir
into the sauce.

Navarin of lamb with turned vegetables

1½ lbs. neck fillets of lamb • 3 carrots, peeled • 3 turnips, peeled • 8 new potatoes • 1 garlic clove • 4 shallots, peeled • 1 tbsp. sunflower oil • 1 tbsp. all-purpose flour • 1½ cups white wine • 1½ cups tomato sauce • 2 sprigs rosemary

SERVES 4

Traditionally this French ragout was made with mutton and baby spring vegetables. Turning the vegetables gives the dish a grander finished look but if you are short of time simply cut the vegetables into even-sized pieces.

1. Preheat the oven to 325° F. Cut the lamb into 1-inch pieces. Cut the carrots, turnips, and potatoes into 2-inch pieces and with a turning knife, trim into barrel-shaped pieces. Finely chop the garlic.

2. Heat the oil in a large Dutch oven and brown the meat in batches, 3–4 minutes. Transfer to a plate. Add the carrots, turnips, potatoes, and shallots and brown all over, 5 minutes.

3. Return the meat and add the garlic and flour and stir well, cooking 1 minute. Stir in the wine, tomato sauce, and rosemary sprigs. Season well and bring to a boil. Then take off the heat, cover, and cook in the oven, 2 hours.

The hooked shape of the turning knife makes it easy to create professional-looking barrel-shaped vegetables.

Loin of pork braised in milk with vegetables

1 large onion • 1 bulb fennel • 1 small celeriac • 2 garlic cloves • 2 tbsp. sunflower oil •
3 lbs. boned loin of pork • 2 cups milk • 6 sage leaves

SERVES 4

In this recipe, the milk curdles during cooking, resulting
in a delicious creamy sauce. The vegetables are
meltingly tender and full of meaty flavor.

1. Preheat the oven to 325° F. Roughly slice the onion and fennel
and place in a large Dutch oven. Peel the celeriac and cut into thick
strips. Thickly slice the garlic. Add these to the onion and fennel
and pour in the oil. Mix well and fry the vegetables, 15 minutes.

2. Remove any skin and fat from the pork loin and place on top of
the vegetables. Pour over the milk and season well.

3. Finely chop the sage leaves and stir in. Cover and cook in the
oven, 1¾–2 hours. Thickly slice the meat and serve with the
vegetables and sauce.

Danish meatballs with tomato sauce

1 onion • 1 garlic clove • 1 slice bacon • 1 small bunch parsley • 4 tbsp. sunflower oil •
2 oz. white bread (about 2 slices), crusts removed • 6 tbsp. milk • 1 lb. ground pork •
½ lb. ground beef • ½ tsp. ground ginger • ½ tsp. grated nutmeg • 1 egg, beaten
For the tomato sauce • 2 14-oz cans chopped tomatoes • 2 tbsp. tomato ketchup •
3 bay leaves • 1 tsp. sugar • 1 tsp. dried mixed herbs

SERVES 6

Scandinavian meatballs are often made with just
ground pork but the combination of both pork and beef
is even better.

1. Cut the onion in half and put in a food processor with the garlic,
bacon, and parsley, and blend until finely chopped. Heat 1 tbsp. oil
in a small pan and fry the mixture 5 minutes then let cool. Soak the
bread in the milk, 5 minutes. Preheat the oven to 375° F.

2. Put the pork and beef in a large mixing bowl and add the cooled
onion mixture. Squeeze out any excess milk from the bread and
add to the bowl along with the spices and egg. Season very well
and mix everything together. With floured hands, shape into sixteen
meatballs.

3. Heat the remaining oil in a skillet and brown the meatballs in
batches, 5–6 minutes. Transfer to a large ovenproof dish and bake,
25 minutes.

4. Place all the ingredients for the tomato sauce in a saucepan
and bring to a boil. Simmer until thick and reduced, 25 minutes.
Serve the meatballs on a platter with the tomato sauce on the side.

Spanish pork with tomatoes and chorizo

2 ¾ lbs. belly of pork, in one piece • 2 onions • 4 garlic cloves • 2 tbsp. sunflower oil • 7 oz. chorizo sausage, skin removed • 1 tbsp. pimentón or paprika • 28-oz. can chopped tomatoes • ½ cup white wine • 2 bay leaves • small bunch parsley

SERVES 6

This is a spicy, earthy dish from Spain. It is slow-cooked until the meat is on the point of disintegrating, and the sauce is heavy and rich. Pimentón is a smoked paprika that is stocked in some supermarkets and in gourmet specialty stores. It gives the dish its authentic flavor.

1. Preheat the oven to 300° F. Cut the pork into ½-inch pieces with a large chopping knife. Finely chop the onions and garlic.

2. Heat the oil in a large Dutch oven and brown the meat in batches. Transfer to a bowl. Fry the onions and garlic until browned, 10 minutes. Roughly chop the chorizo, add to the Dutch oven, and fry 5 minutes. Stir in the pimentón.

3. Return the meat to the Dutch oven and add the tomatoes, wine, and bay leaves. Cover and cook in the oven, 3 hours.

4. Finely chop the parsley and stir in before serving.

Carpaccio of beef

1 ¼ lbs. piece finest quality fillet of beef • 1 egg • 1 tbsp. Dijon mustard •
½ cup peanut oil or light olive oil • 2 tbsp. heavy cream

SERVES 4

The meat in this recipe is served uncooked, and thus is imperative that it be fresh and of the finest quality.

1. Wrap the beef fillet in plastic wrap and put in the freezer to firm up, about 20 minutes. This will make it easier to slice. Put on a board and with a chef's knife cut across the grain into very fine slivers.

2. Place 2–3 slivers in between plastic wrap and lightly tenderize with a rolling pin so they are paper-thin. Continue with the remaining pieces.

3. Arrange in a single layer over four large dinner plates. Add plenty of black pepper.

4. Put the egg and mustard in a food processor and add a pinch of salt. Blend for a few seconds. While the motor is running slowly pour in the oil, as if you were making mayonnaise. The sauce should have a pouring consistency. Add the cream and blend for a couple of seconds. Transfer to a jug and serve either on the side or drizzled over the beef.

Note: Recipes using uncooked meat should be avoided by infants, the elderly, pregnant women, and anyone with a compromised immune system.

Fillet of beef with mushroom and Madeira sauce

1 ¾ lbs. piece fillet of beef • 2 tbsp. olive oil • 2 tbsp. black peppercorns
For the sauce • 8 shallots, peeled • 2 tbsp. butter • 2 cups mixed wild mushrooms or
portobello mushrooms • ½ cup Madeira wine • 1 ½ cups chicken broth • 3 tbsp. sour
cream • 1 small bunch chives

SERVES 4

**To make this dish truly special, use a selection of mixed
wild mushrooms, often available from farmers' markets.
Otherwise, use a flavorful cultivated variety, such as
portobello, or dried wild mushrooms which can be soaked.**

1. Preheat the oven to 425° F. Trim the beef removing any fat and
sinews, and brush with the olive oil. Crush the peppercorns in a
mortar and pestle then pat onto the surface of the beef. Place in a
roasting pan and roast, 35–40 minutes. Add on an extra 5–10
minutes if you want medium to well-done beef.

2. For the sauce, finely chop the shallots. Melt the butter in a large
skillet and fry the shallots until soft and golden, 15 minutes. Chop
the mushrooms, add to the skillet, and fry an additional 10 minutes.

3. Turn the heat up, pour in the Madeira, and reduce the liquid by
half—there should be very little liquid remaining. Pour in the chicken
broth and again reduce by half. The reduction is important as it will
give the sauce a full concentrated flavor so don't skip this part.

4. Stir in the sour cream, taste, and adjust the seasoning. Snip the
chives with kitchen scissors and stir into the sauce.

5. Allow the beef to rest before slicing, 15 minutes. Serve with the
sauce on the side.

Steak tartare

1 lb. piece finest quality fillet of beef • 1 small onion • 1 small bunch parsley • 1 tbsp. capers • 1 tsp. Worcestershire sauce • 4 egg yolks • 2 tbsp. peanut or sunflower oil • crisp lettuce

SERVES 4

Because the meat in this recipe is uncooked, its freshness must not be in question. Shop where you can guarantee quality produce for a delicious result.

1. Finely chop the steak with a sharp knife or Chinese cleaver and put in a bowl. Finely chop the onion, parsley, and capers with a mezzaluna and mix with the meat. Stir in the remaining ingredients and season lightly.

2. Pat into four hamburger shapes and garnish with crisp lettuce. Serve with warm toast or sautéed potatoes.

Note: Recipes using uncooked meat should be avoided by infants, the elderly, pregnant women, and anyone with a compromised immune system.

Shredded beef with chili vegetable stir-fry

1 lb. piece fillet of beef • 3 tbsp. soy sauce • 1 tbsp. sesame oil • 1 tsp. Thai fish
sauce (nam pla) • 2 tsp. sugar • For the stir-fry • 2-inch fresh ginger, peeled • 2 garlic
cloves • 4 scallions • 3 red chilis, deseeded • 1 head Chinese cabbage • 1 red bell
pepper, deseeded • 1 yellow bell pepper, deseeded • 2 cups broccoli florets • ½ cup
haricots verts (thin green beans) • 1 tbsp. sunflower oil • 3 tbsp. soy sauce • 4 tbsp.
dry sherry • ⅓ cup cashew nuts • 1 tbsp. sesame oil

SERVES 4

**Finely sliced beef works wonderfully with a selection of
vegetables in this spicy stir-fry.**

1. Using a Chinese cleaver, slice the beef into very fine shavings.
Mix the soy sauce, fish sauce, sesame oil, and sugar together in a
shallow dish and stir in the beef. Allow to marinate a few minutes.

2. Get all the vegetables ready before starting to stir-fry. Finely chop
the ginger, garlic, and scallions. Finely shred the red chilis and
Chinese cabbage. Slice the red and yellow peppers. Cut the broccoli
into tiny pieces and halve the green beans.

3. Heat the oil in a wok and stir-fry the ginger, garlic, scallions, and
chilis, 3–4 minutes. Add the peppers and stir-fry, an additional 3–4
minutes.

4. Add the broccoli and beans to the wok along with the soy sauce
and sherry and stir-fry, 5–6 minutes. Add the Chinese cabbage and
cashew nuts and continue to cook, 3–4 minutes. Stir in the sesame
oil. Spoon into a large serving bowl and keep warm while you cook
the beef.

5. Heat the wok and when it is hot add the marinated beef. Stir-fry,
3–4 minutes. Arrange on top of the stir-fried vegetables and serve
immediately.

jointing a chicken

Of course it's convenient to buy your chicken already jointed, but having a whole bird in the refrigerator or freezer gives you a much wider choice of ways to cook it. You can cook it whole as a straightforward oven roast or joint the chicken to make anything from a tagine to marinated chicken pieces for the grill.

Here the chicken has been divided into eight pieces, but if you prefer larger pieces, simply keep the breast and leg pieces whole to make four.

 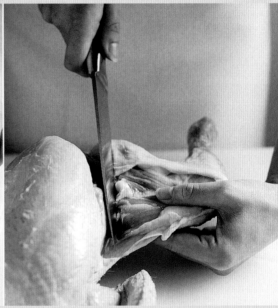

step 1 Wipe the inside and outside of the chicken with a wad of moistened paper towels. Put chicken on a chopping board and, using a sharp chef's knife, cut the wing tips off at the joint.

step 2 With the breast side up, pull a leg away from the body and cut through the ball and socket joint. Remove from the carcass then repeat with the other leg.

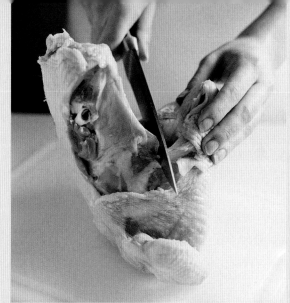

step 3 Holding the chicken sideways toward you, neck end down, cut through the ribs to separate the lower part of the breast and the wings from the lower body.

step 4 Cut the breast in half along the breastbone. You can use the chef's knife, but poultry shears or even sharp kitchen scissors are easiest to snip through the bone.

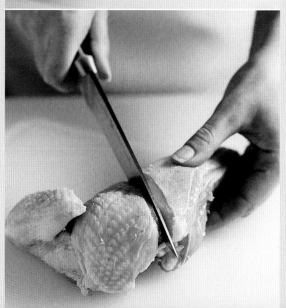

step 5 Divide the breast in half again widthwise, behind the wing. Divide the leg from the drumstick. You now have four breast pieces, two drumsticks, and two thighs.

Chicken and orange tagine

4 lbs. chicken • 2 tbsp. butter • 1 tbsp. olive oil • 2 onions • large pinch saffron powder •
2 tsp. cumin seeds • pinch chili flakes • ½ cinnamon stick • 1 orange • 3 garlic cloves •
1 cup chicken broth • ½ cup fresh orange juice • couscous to serve

SERVES 6

A tagine is in fact the vessel in which Moroccans cook a
lot of their food. It has a shallow base and a pointed lid.
But don't worry if you don't have one—a heavy-based
Dutch oven serves just as well.

1. Cut the chicken into eight pieces—four breast pieces, two with
wings and two without, two drumsticks, and two thighs.

2. Preheat the oven to 350° F. Melt the butter with the oil in a
tagine and brown the chicken joints, 5–6 minutes. Transfer to a
plate with a slotted spoon.

3. Slice the onions into eighths, add to the tagine and brown, 5
minutes. Add the saffron, cumin seeds, chili flakes, and cinnamon
stick and cook, 2 minutes. Return the chicken to the tagine.

4. Peel the orange and cut into chunks. Roughly chop the garlic
and stir both into the tagine. Pour in the stock and orange juice,
bring to a boil, and season well. Cover and cook in the oven, 1¼
hours. Serve with couscous.

Chicken satay with peanut dip

skinless chicken breasts • 1 red chili, deseeded • 1 garlic clove • 1-inch fresh ginger, peeled • 1 tbsp. dark soy sauce • 1 tsp. rice wine vinegar • 1 tsp. sesame oil
For the dip • ⅔ cup natural roasted peanuts • 1 garlic clove • pinch chili flakes • 1 tbsp. dark soy sauce • 2 tsp. brown sugar • ½ cup coconut milk

SERVES 4 as an appetizer

These spicy sticks make the best canapés. Great for dipping!

1. Cut the chicken breasts into long thin strips with a Chinese cleaver and put in a mixing bowl. Finely chop the chili, garlic, and ginger and add to the chicken. Stir in the soy sauce, rice wine vinegar, and sesame oil and allow to marinate, 30 minutes. Thread onto bamboo skewers that have been soaked in water, 30 minutes.

2. For the dip, put the peanuts in a food processor and blend until roughly chopped. Transfer to a small saucepan. Finely chop the garlic and add to the pan with the chili flakes, soy sauce, and brown sugar. Mix well and heat gently, stirring in the coconut milk after a couple of minutes. Continue to cook, 3–4 minutes. Put the chicken satay under a hot broiler and broil, 5–6 minutes, turning the sticks over to ensure that all the sides are cooked. Serve with the warm peanut dip.

Chicken liver pâté

1½ lbs. chicken livers which will yield about 1 lb. • 1 small onion • 1 garlic clove • 1¾ sticks butter • 4 tbsp. heavy cream • 2 tbsp. Marsala wine

SERVES 6 as a starter

Classic pâtés never go out of style. This truly great version is full of flavor with a velvety smooth texture.

1. Carefully prepare the chicken livers, cutting away any tough stringy tubes or dark discolored patches. Finely chop the onion and garlic. Melt about half the butter in a skillet and fry the onion and garlic until soft, 15 minutes. Add the chicken livers and fry until they feel firm, 8–10 minutes. Season with a little salt and plenty of pepper. Spoon the contents of the skillet in a food processor. Add the remaining butter, cream, and Marsala, and blend until smooth. Pass the mixture through a fine sieve and spoon into a serving bowl. Chill for a couple of hours until firm. Serve with warm toast.

Mu shu duck

2 ½ lbs. duck • 1 garlic clove • 2 tbsp. hoisin sauce • 1 tbsp. sweet soy sauce • 1 tbsp. honey • ½ cucumber • 1 small bunch scallions • 12 store-bought Chinese pancakes • 6 tbsp. hoisin sauce

SERVES 4 as an appetizer

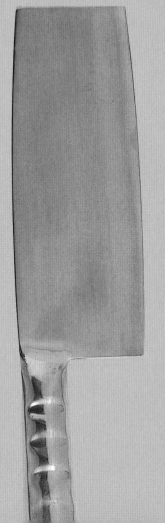

You will need Chinese pancakes for this dish which are available in Asian supermarkets—usually in the freezer compartments.

1. Dry the duck well and allow to hang in a cool, dry place, 12 hours. Preheat the oven to 400° F. Prick the duck skin with a fork. Sit on a rack in a large roasting pan and roast about, 1½ hours.

2. Mince the garlic and mix with the hoisin sauce, soy sauce, and honey. Halfway through cooking the duck, remove from the oven and brush all over with the glaze. Return to the oven and complete the cooking.

3. Halve the cucumber lengthwise and scrape out the seeds. Halve again widthwise and with a Chinese cleaver, slice the cucumber very finely. Finely shred the scallions.

4. Let the duck rest before carving, 15 minutes. Put duck on a chopping board and with a chef's knife remove the legs. Pick away the meat and finely shred. Carve slices from both of the breasts and shred finely.

5. To serve, put the meat in the center of a serving plate and arrange piles of the cucumber and scallions around it. Steam the pancakes in a clean dishtowel, 1–2 minutes, and arrange on a plate. Let people help themselves, spreading a little hoisin sauce over a pancake and filling with duck and shreds of cucumber and scallion.

boning a chicken

This task requires a certain amount of patience, but once you've begun, all will become clear and straightforward. And of course, the finished result, when stuffed, makes a spectacular centerpiece for that special occasion, or even if you just want to treat the family. Boned and stuffed chicken is a tidy, compact dish which can be easily carved into slices. Don't try the technique on a chicken weighing less than 4 pounds, as the effort isn't really worth the result.

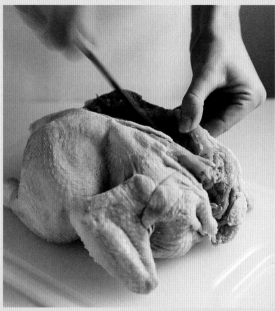 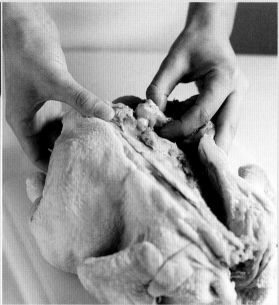

step 1 Cut off the "pope's nose" (or tailpiece) and the wing tips. Lay the chicken on a board, on its breast. Cut along the backbone, with a boning knife, starting from the neck.

step 2 With the tip of the knife pressed against the rib cage, loosen the meat, pulling it away. Scrape away the meat around the thighbone joint and twist to pop out the ball joint.

step 3 Loosen the meat away from the base of the rib cage. Scrape the meat from the wing joint and twist to free the joint from the socket. Scrape the breast meat almost away from the carcass.

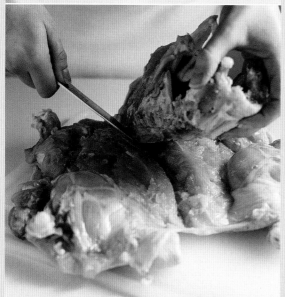

step 4 Repeat the boning on other side. Using the knife, carefully lift the carcass from the meat, being extra-careful not to pierce the thin skin that runs along the breastbone.

step 5 Scrape the meat from the thigh bones and pull inside out to remove completely. Do the same for the wing bone. Trim away the white tendons. Now you have a lovely boneless chicken for cooking.

Chicken with olive, bacon, and parsley stuffing

4 lbs. chicken • 1 onion • 3 garlic cloves • 1 stick celery • 2 tbsp. olive oil •
5 oz. bacon, in one piece • ½ cup pitted black olives • 1 small bunch parsley •
6 thyme sprigs • 1 cup bread crumbs • 2 tsp. grated lemon peel • 1 egg,
beaten • 2 tbsp. butter, softened • ½ cup white wine • ½ cup chicken broth

SERVES 4–6

The aromatic stuffing lends a delicious moistness to the boned chicken in this recipe.

1. Bone the chicken and chill in the refrigerator until ready for stuffing.

2. Preheat the oven to 400° F. For the stuffing, finely chop the onion, celery, and garlic. Heat the oil in a skillet and fry the vegetables until browned, 15 minutes. Cut the bacon into cubes, add to the skillet, and fry, 5 minutes. Remove from the heat and cool.

3. Roughly chop the olives, parsley, and thyme and mix with the bread crumbs and lemon peel in a mixing bowl. Stir in the cooled onion mixture. Pour in the beaten egg, season, and mix well.

4. Place the stuffing mixture down the center of the boned chicken, covering the breasts. Pull the sides up and across to cover the stuffing and tie with string to secure.

5. Put in a roasting pan and smear the surface with the softened butter. Roast until a skewer inserted into the center for 10 seconds feels very hot, 1¼–1½ hours. Transfer to a plate and keep warm.

6. To make the gravy, pour off any excess fat from the roasting pan and deglaze with the wine and broth, stirring to loosen any residue. Pour into a jug and serve with the chicken.

Spicy chicken sausages

1 onion • 2 garlic cloves • 2 tbsp. butter • 1 tbsp. paprika • 1½ lbs. boned chicken thighs • 2 red chilis, deseeded • 1 small bunch parsley • 10 thyme sprigs • 1 cup fresh white bread crumbs • 1 egg, beaten • 4 tbsp. sunflower oil

SERVES 4

Serve these flavorful little gems on a bed of juicy tomatoes. They beat store-bought ones hands down!

1. Finely chop the onion and garlic. Melt the butter in a skillet and fry the onion and garlic, 5 minutes. Add the paprika and fry, 1 minute. Take off the heat and let cool.

2. Place the boneless chicken thighs in a food processor and process a few seconds until the meat is finely chopped. Don't over process or it will become a paste. Transfer to a mixing bowl.

3. Finely chop the chili, parsley, and thyme with a mezzaluna, and mix into the ground chicken with the cooled onion mixture and bread crumbs. Add the beaten egg and stir well. Season well.

4. Divide the mixture into twelve balls and roll into sausages. Heat the oil in a skillet and fry the sausages, turning regularly, until browned and cooked through, 15–20 minutes.

fish

fish introduction

Fish is a wonderfully various category of meat. There are subtle differences in flavor depending on which branch of the family it comes from, its water environment, its diet, etc. The real beauty of fish is its texture—the delicate fineness of flesh found in flat fish like John Dory and flounder, the intriguing flakes that effortlessly slip off the bones of a skate wing, the almost steak-like texture of tuna and swordfish, or the generous chunks of flesh that separate out as you cut into a juicy cod fillet.

Fish is a fantastic food to cook—it takes minutes in the pan, is meltingly tender, and it's good for you too. Most supermarkets now operate great fish counters where the quality and freshness have been taken care of, so all you have to do is choose. Look for bright eyes, red gills, glistening skin, and a rigid body. If anything smells remotely off or not "of the sea," don't buy it. Keep an eye out for bargains too— lesser cuts like salmon tails are very cheap and

taste just the same as the more expensive cuts. Either use the fish the day you buy it—it will keep in the refrigerator until the next day—or package it up straightaway in a plastic bag and store in the freezer for no more than a month.

Your fishmonger will prepare your fish for you. Watch carefully what he does and when you try filleting for yourself, you'll be ahead of the game. Filleting at home is easy, as long as you're using the right knife. It's well worth buying a special fish filleting knife. These knives have sharp, flexible blades which won't tear into the flesh—fish flesh is so delicate that a clumsy knife can easily ruin it. If you don't think it's worth investing in one for filleting alone, this type of knife is also very good for all kinds of slicing, particularly when you are slicing smoked salmon or tomatoes very thinly. The large Chinese or Japanese cleavers are also good for chopping or slicing meatier fish like tuna or salmon.

filleting and skinning fish

Flat fish like lemon sole (shown here) and flounder are easy to fillet. The same general principles apply to round fish like cod and red snapper, which are not shown here.

Before you start, make sure your filleting knife is very sharp and have a little pot of salt ready (ordinary table salt which has fine grains, not rock salt or sea salt, as it won't stick to your fingers) to help you get a vice-like grip on the fish's slippery skin. And once you have done one fillet, the rest will be a pushover.

step 1 Lay the lemon sole on a chopping board, dark side up, and remove the head using a filleting knife. Cut down the length of the fish, through the center.

step 2 Insert the knife at an angle of about 45 degrees and with short strokes, pry one fillet from the rib bones. Repeat on the other dark side and remove the other fillet.

step 3 Once you have removed the two fillets from the dark side, turn the fish over and remove the fillets from the white side in the same way as before.

step 4 Using a pair of sharp kitchen scissors, trim the fin off each fillet. To skin, lay each fillet on the board, skin-side down, tail end toward you.

step 5 Insert the knife between the skin and the flesh, then, holding the skin tightly (dip your fingers in salt to get a better grip), move the knife away from you, keeping it flat.

Sole stuffed with asparagus with shallot sauce

3 whole lemon sole • 2 small zucchini • 8 baby asparagus spears • 2 tbsp. butter • For the sauce • 3 oz. shallots • 2 tbsp. butter • ½ cup white wine or vermouth • 1 cup heavy cream • small bunch parsley, finely chopped

SERVES 4

A combination of deliciously delicate flavors, this sophisticated dish is easier to make than it looks!

1. Cut each fish into four fillets. Preheat the oven to 350° F.

2. Using a chef's knife, cut the zucchini in half widthwise then into julienne strips. Melt the butter in a skillet and fry the zucchini, 4–5 minutes. Remove with a slotted spoon and set aside.

3. Fry the asparagus in the butter, 4–5 minutes, then mix with the zucchini and allow to cool.

4. Lay the sole fillets out onto a board. Place a small handful of the vegetables on the wide end of the fillet and roll up. Carefully place on a greased baking tray and cook in the oven, 12–15 minutes.

5. To make the sauce, finely chop the shallots. Melt the butter in a small pan and fry shallots 10 minutes. Add the wine or vermouth and simmer until there is very little liquid remaining, 3–4 minutes. Pour in the cream, season, and simmer, 3–4 minutes. Finely chop the parsley and stir into the sauce just before serving.

Marinated grilled fish with aioli

2 sprigs rosemary • 2 tbsp. fresh lemon juice • 6 tbsp. olive oil • 1 ½ lbs. firm white fish fillets, skinned, e.g., monkfish, orange roughy • 12 large raw peeled shrimp • fresh bay leaves For the aioli • 3 garlic cloves • pinch salt • 2 egg yolks • 2 tsp. white wine vinegar • 1 tsp. English mustard powder • 1 cup light olive oil

SERVES 4

These fish skewers give an exotic flavor to your grill. A true aioli is made with extra-virgin olive oil, but I think the flavor is a bit overpowering. So substitute a lighter olive oil if you prefer

1. For the aioli, put the garlic cloves in a mortar and pestle with the salt and pound to a paste. Mix in the egg yolks, white wine vinegar, and mustard powder, and pound again. Drop by drop add the olive oil, pounding to emulsify the mixture. Continue until all the oil is used. If the aioli becomes too thick mix in 1 tsp. warm water. Chill until ready to serve.

2. For the marinade, remove the leaves from the rosemary stalks and finely chop. Put in a shallow dish and mix in the lemon juice and oil.

3. Cut the fish into 2-inch chunks and place in the marinade along with the shrimp. Leave 20 minutes.

4. Thread pieces of fish and shrimp onto metal skewers with the odd bay leaf in between. Just before season well and cook over hot coals, 8–10 minutes. Serve with the aioli on the side.

Harissa-coated monkfish medallions with fruity couscous

12 oz. couscous • 2 scallions • 1 small bunch cilantro • 6 dried apricots • ⅓ cup almonds, toasted •
½ cup raisins • 1 tbsp. fresh lemon juice • 4 tbsp. olive oil • 1½ lbs. monkfish tails
For the harissa • 4 dried chilis • 2 fresh red chilis • 2 garlic cloves • 2 tsp. cumin seeds • 2 tsp.
cilantro seeds • 2 tsp. caraway seeds • 1 tbsp. fresh lemon juice • 3 tbsp. olive oil

SERVES 4

Harissa is a fiery red chili paste from North Africa which is used to flavor a great many of the region's dishes. This recipe makes more than you will need for the monkfish—it's barely worth making less—but it keeps for about a month in the refrigerator.

1. For the harissa, soak the dried chilis in boiling water, 30 minutes. Preheat the oven to 400° F. Put the fresh chilis in an oven dish and roast, 20 minutes.

2. Remove the stalks from the dried and fresh chilis and put, whole, in the bowl of the food processor. Add the remaining harissa ingredients and blend until smooth. Spoon into a jar and chill until needed.

3. Put the couscous in a bowl and pour over 1½ cups boiling water. Cover with plastic wrap, leave for 15 minutes then fluff up with a fork.

4. Finely chop the scallions and cilantro and stir into the couscous. Roughly chop the apricots and almonds and add to the bowl along with the raisins, lemon juice, and 3 tbsp. oil. Season well and transfer to a serving dish.

5. Cut the monkfish into 2-inch medallions and put in a mixing bowl. Stir in 4 tsp. of harissa and mix to coat every piece with the paste. Heat the remaining oil in a large skillet and fry the fish, 2–3 minutes on each side. Arrange on top of the couscous and pour any pan juices over the top.

Thai fish cakes

1 lb. white fish fillets, skinned · 4 kaffir lime leaves · 2 tbsp. Thai green paste (see page 69) · 1 tbsp. Thai fish sauce (nam pla) · 1 tbsp. dark soy sauce · 1 small bunch cilantro · 1 small handful haricots verts (thin green beans) · oil for shallow frying · For the dipping sauce · 1 red chili · 1 small bunch mint · 2 tbsp. sugar · 6 tbsp. rice wine vinegar

SERVES 4

Get that authentic Thai flavor by using genuine Thai ingredients bought from Asian supermarkets.

1. Put all the ingredients for the fish cakes—except the beans—in a food processor and blend until smooth. Transfer to a mixing bowl.

2. Very finely chop the beans and mix into the fish cakes with a little salt.

3. With wet hands divide the mixture into eight balls and shape into patties. Chill while you make the dipping sauce.

4. Finely chop the chili and mint. In a small bowl mix the sugar into the vinegar until dissolved and stir in the chopped chili and mint.

5. Heat the oil in a skillet and fry the fish cakes, 4–5 minutes on each side. Serve hot with the dipping sauce.

Roast cod with fried gremolata bread crumbs

2 garlic cloves • 1 large bunch parsley • 4 tsp. grated lemon peel • 2 cups bread crumbs, made from stale ciabatta • 2 tbsp. olive oil • 4 thick skinless cod fillets, about 7 oz. each • 1 ½ tsp. Dijon mustard

SERVES 4

1. Preheat the oven to 400° F. Put the garlic cloves and parsley on a board and finely chop with a mezzaluna. Put in a bowl and stir in lemon peel, bread crumbs, and olive oil.

2. Toast in a skillet until crisp and golden, 4–5 minutes.

3. Put the cod fillets on an oiled baking tray. Lightly brush with the Dijon mustard and pat the bread crumbs over the top of the fish. Bake until the fish feels firm to the touch, 10 –12 minutes.

Gremolata, a parsley, lemon, and garlic mixture, is traditionally sprinkled over the Italian dish Osso Bucco. Here it is mixed with lemon peel, bread crumbs, and olive oil then fried and used to coat juicy cod fillets.

Charbroiled salmon with red onion marmalade

5 red onions • 4 tbsp. olive oil • 3 tbsp. balsamic vinegar • 2 tbsp. brown sugar • 2 tbsp. butter • 2 lbs. salmon fillet, in one piece • 1 tbsp. black peppercorns

SERVES 4

1. With a large chef's knife, finely slice the onion. Heat the oil in a large nonstick skillet and add the onion. Stir to coat in the oil, cover, and fry, 20 minutes. Stir now and then to prevent the onions from sticking. Add the vinegar and sugar, and fry uncovered, an additional 20 minutes. Stir in the butter.

2. While the onions are cooking, prepare the salmon. Skin the salmon fillet with a fish knife (see page 11) and cut into four pieces. Grind the peppercorns in a mortar and pestle until quite fine and press onto the upper side of each salmon fillet.

3. Heat a ridged skillet until smoking. Add the salmon and cook, 3–4 minutes each side. Serve with the red onion marmalade.

This sweet and sour marmalade is a great foil for the oily salmon. It also makes a wonderful relish for a mature, spicy cheddar cheese. It takes a fair time to cook but can be made in advance and heated up.

Red snapper with julienne of vegetables and chive butter

3 stalks celery · 2 carrots, peeled · 1 bulb fennel · 4-oz. can baby corn · 2 tbsp. butter · 4 snapper fillets, about 7 oz. each · 1 tbsp. melted butter
For the chive butter · 1 stick butter, softened · 1 small bunch chives · 1 tbsp. Dijon mustard

SERVES 4

Red snapper is a wonderfully meaty yet delicate fish, commonly found in Caribbean cuisine but increasingly popular around the world.

1. For the chive butter, put the butter, chives, and Dijon mustard in the small bowl of a food processor and blend until smooth. Put in a large piece of plastic wrap and roll into a cylinder. Chill for at least 30 minutes. Cut into four ½-inch thick disks.

2. Cut the celery and carrots into 3-inch long pieces and slice into fine julienne strips. Top and tail the fennel and slice into fine strips. Quarter the baby corn lengthwise.

3. Melt the butter in a skillet and gently fry the vegetables, 8–10 minutes.

4. Brush the snapper fillets with the melted butter, season, and place on a baking tray. Broil under a hot broiler, 3–4 minutes each side. Put a pile of vegetables onto each plate and arrange a snapper fillet on top. Place a disk of chive butter onto each fillet and serve immediately.

Tuna and salmon sushi

1 cup Japanese sushi rice • 1 tbsp. rice vinegar • 1 tbsp. sake • ½ tsp. salt • 3 oz. fresh tuna • 2 oz. fresh salmon • 1 tsp. wasabi paste • 3 sheets nori seaweed • soy sauce for dipping • pickled ginger for garnish

SERVES 4–6 as a starter

Real Japanese sushi is a snip to make, provided you have the proper ingredients. Get them from your local Asian supermarket. The end result looks so neat and pretty— and tastes even better!

1. Put the rice in a saucepan and pour over enough water to stand about ½-inch above the rice. Add the rice vinegar, sake, and salt and cover. Bring to a boil then turn the heat down to barely simmering. Cook until the rice has absorbed all the liquid, 15–20 minutes. Spoon onto a greased baking tray and cool.

2. With a Japanese cleaver cut the salmon and tuna into thin matchstick pieces.

3. Spread a piece of plastic wrap onto a board and place a sheet of nori on top. Brush with water to moisten a little. Spread the rice over two thirds of the nori, leaving the farthest bit away from you uncovered.

4. Brush a horizontal central strip of rice with the merest hint of wasabi paste. Lay half the matchstick pieces of tuna across this. Using the plastic wrap, roll up the nori starting nearest to you and rolling away. Press a little to form a neat roll and cut into four or five pieces. Serve with extra wasabi paste, soy sauce for dipping, and a bowl of pickled ginger.

Warm smoked salmon with spaghetti vegetables

1 large leek • 1 large zucchini • 2 large carrots • small bunch chives • 2 tbsp. sunflower oil • ¾ lb. smoked salmon • lemon wedges to garnish

SERVES 4 as a starter

This elegant starter can be prepared a couple of hours in advance and then simply stir-fried at the last minute.

1. Trim the leek and cut into fine strips lengthwise. Set aside.

2. Top and tail the zucchini and cut into long thin "spaghetti" strips.

3. Peel the carrots and cut into even-sized strips. Bring a pan of water to a boil and blanch the carrots, 3 minutes. Drain and refresh under cold water. Finely chop the chives. Warm four plates in a low oven.

4. Heat the oil in a wok and stir-fry the leeks, 2–3 minutes. Add the zucchini and carrot and stir-fry, an additional 3–4 minutes. Season and mix in the chives.

5. Remove the plates from the oven and lay strips of smoked salmon over each. The heat from the plates will gently warm the salmon. Top with a pile of vegetables and garnish each plate with a wedge of lemon.

New England clam chowder

3 lbs. fresh clams • 1 onion • 3 slices bacon • 2 medium-sized potatoes, peeled • 2 tbsp. butter • 4 sprigs fresh thyme • 1 bay leaf • 2 ½ cups milk

SERVES 4

Chowder supposedly derives its name from the French cooking pot—*chaudière*—which French settlers brought over to Canada. Unlike Manhattan chowder, which is tomato-based, the New England chowder is a creamy concoction of potatoes, onions, bacon, and clams.

1. Wash and scrub the clams. Discard any that refuse to open after a sharp tap. Pour enough water to come up to ½ inch in a large saucepan and add the clams. Cover with a tight-fitting lid and bring to a boil. Cook 2 minutes then drain, reserving 1 ¼ cups cooking liquor. Remove the clams from their shells, discarding any that are shut.

2. Finely chop the onion and bacon and dice the potatoes. Melt the butter in a large pan and fry the onion, bacon, and potatoes, 5 minutes.

3. Add the thyme sprigs, bay leaf, and milk. Pour in the reserved liquor and simmer the soup until the potatoes are on the point of breaking up, 20–25 minutes. Remove the sprigs of thyme and bay leaf. Season well and stir in the clams. Simmer 1 minute to heat through.

Grapefruit, shrimp, and avocado salad

1 garlic clove • 2 tsp. grated lemon peel • 2 tbsp. fresh lemon juice • 2 tbsp. olive oil • 1 lb. raw, peeled shrimp • 2 grapefruit • 2 avocados • small bunch chives

SERVES 4

These three flavors complement each other so well, making a delicious salad to eat on its own or as an accompaniment.

1. Pound the garlic in a mortar and pestle with the lemon peel and juice and 1 tbsp. of the oil. Spoon into a bowl and add the shrimp. Stir and allow to marinate, 30 minutes.

2. Peel and segment the grapefruit with a serrated fruit knife (see page 10) and arrange in a salad bowl. Halve the avocados, remove the stone, and peel away the skin. Thinly slice and carefully arrange among the grapefruit segments.

3. Heat the remaining oil in a skillet and fry the shrimp, until firm and pink all over, 3–4 minutes. Let cool then spoon over the salad. Snip the chives with a pair of kitchen scissors and scatter over the salad. Chill until ready to serve.

Stir-fried shrimp with crispy seaweed

1 lb. spring greens • oil for deep frying • ¼ tsp. salt • ½ tsp. sugar • 1 garlic clove • 1-inch piece fresh ginger, peeled • 1 green chili, deseeded • 4 scallions • 1 tbsp. peanut oil • 1 lb. raw, peeled shrimp • 1 tbsp. soy sauce

SERVES 4

Chinese crispy seaweed isn't really made of seaweed, but deep-fried greens. When spring greens are unavailable use Savoy or spring cabbage.

1. Slice the greens very finely with a Chinese cleaver. Heat a deep-fryer to 375° F. Fry the greens in small batches until deep green and crispy, 20–30 seconds. Drain on paper towels and sprinkle with the salt and sugar. Keep warm while you cook the shrimp.

2. Finely chop the garlic, ginger, chili, and scallions. Heat the oil in a wok and add the garlic mixture. Stir-fry for 2–3 minutes. Add the shrimp and soy sauce and cook until the shrimp are firm and pink all over, 2–3 minutes. Serve with the crispy "seaweed."

Spaghetti with squid and roasted chili

¾ lb. cleaned squid • 4 red chilis • 2 garlic cloves • 1 small bunch parsley • 6 tbsp. olive oil • 1 lb. spaghetti • 1 tbsp. fresh lemon juice

SERVES 4

The combination of squid, roasted chili, garlic, and herbs is a winner. For a lighter meal, toss the cooked squid into a bowl of salad leaves instead of pasta.

1. Chop the squid tubes into 1-inch pieces, keeping the tentacles whole. Put in a mixing bowl.

2. Broil the chilis on a baking tray under a preheated medium broiler until the skins are charred, 6–8 minutes.

3. Cool then peel off the burnt skins. Scrape away the seeds and finely chop the flesh. Finely chop the garlic and parsley. Mix the chilis, garlic, and parsley with the squid and stir in the olive oil. Season with a little salt.

4. Bring a large pan of salted water to a rolling boil. Cook the pasta until al dente, 10–12 minutes. Drain. About 5 minutes before it is ready, start to cook the squid. Tip the squid mixture into a wok or large skillet and stir-fry over high heat, 3–4 minutes. Add the lemon juice and toss with the drained pasta.

fruit & desserts

fruit & desserts introduction

Whatever the time of year, fruit will always be on the menu. Some seasons are bursting with produce. During the summer months there's a real bounty to choose from—strawberries, raspberries, cherries, peaches, nectarines, and apricots are all there for the

picking, while fall brings its own harvest of apples, pears, blackberries, red and black currants, plums, and quinces. Warm regions provide us with winter sunshine—grapefruit, lemons, clementines, tangerines, and all their various siblings and cousins, oranges, pineapples, and mangoes which have the most superb flavor.

Most fruit needs just a modicum of care when preparing—hulling a strawberry or pitting a cherry doesn't require a knife, but some fruits do. Mangoes, for instance, have a uniquely shaped flat stone which can take some getting used to, and although a pineapple can be simply chopped in wedges and eaten, if you want to use it in a fruit salad, you will need to remove its skin and eyes before you chop it. A serrated fruit knife will prove invaluable too,

especially for preparing oranges, where it is important to remove the skin, white pith, and segments neatly.

Other ingredients you are likely to encounter are chocolate, best chopped with a large cook's knife, and nuts. It's quick to throw nuts into the food processor but beware of over-processing them or they will start to release their oils.

With the recipes in this chapter it's easy to satisfy the sweetest of sweet tooths!

Chocolate and cherry nut slices

7 oz. unsweetened chocolate · 1 stick unsalted butter · ½ cup corn syrup · ¾ lb.
ginger snap cookies · 1 cup candied cherries · ⅔ cup roughly chopped toasted
macadamia nuts

MAKES 8 slices

**These incredibly delicious slices are great served for tea or
dessert. That most superior of nuts, the macadamia, is used
here, although you can substitute them with hazelnuts.**

1. Roughly chop the chocolate and butter with a medium-sized knife and
place in a large bowl with the syrup. Melt by either microwaving on medium, 2
minutes, or set the bowl over a saucepan of simmering water until melted.

2. Place half the cookies in a food processor and process to fine crumbs.
Roughly chop the remaining cookies and add both to the melted chocolate
mixture. Halve the cherries and add with the nuts to the chocolate. Mix really
well so that the cookies, cherries, and nuts are coated in chocolate.

3. Line an 8-inch loose-bottomed cake pan with waxed paper. Spoon in the
chocolate mixture and allow to set in the refrigerator, 2 hours. Remove from
the pan, peel off the paper, and cut into slices.

**chopping chocolate Take a
chef's knife and push down on
the top of the blade, gently
rocking the knife back and
forth. Take it slowly and the
pieces won't fly everywhere.**

Chocolate brioche pudding

14 oz. brioche loaf • 6 tbsp. unsalted butter, softened • 7 oz. unsweetened chocolate •
1 ¼ cups half-and-half • 1 package vanilla pudding • 1 cup milk

SERVES 8

1. With a serrated bread knife cut the crusts off the brioche loaf then cut into ½-inch slices. Grease a 9-inch square gratin dish with a little of the butter then sparingly spread the remaining butter over the brioche. Lay half the slices over the bottom of the dish.

2. Place half the chocolate on a board and roughly chop with a large chef's knife. Sprinkle evenly over the brioche then top with the remaining buttered slices. Finely chop the remaining chocolate. Bring the cream to a boil in a small saucepan, add the chocolate, and stir until melted.

3. Whisk the pudding and milk together and stir in the chocolate cream. Pour over the brioche and allow to soak for 30 minutes. Preheat the oven to 300° F. Place the dish in a bain-marie and cook in the oven, 55 minutes to an hour. It should be firm with a little wobble. Let stand 5 minutes before serving.

This very indulgent, rich pudding is extremely good eaten cold the day after baking. However, it's difficult to keep it around for that long!

Bitter chocolate sorbet

8 oz. unsweetened chocolate • 1 cup sugar • 3 tbsp. cocoa

SERVES 4

1. Put the chocolate in a food processor and blend until finely chopped. Place the sugar and cocoa in a saucepan with 2 cups water and slowly bring to a boil, stirring to dissolve the sugar. Bring to a boil then simmer, 5 minutes.

2. Pour the chocolate syrup into the food processor and run until the mixture is completely smooth and the chocolate has melted. Pour into a shallow container and allow to cool. Once cool, put in the freezer to harden for 2–3 hours. Blend until smooth in the food processor. Return to the container and freeze until hard.

Intensely dark and rich this will satisfy any chocolate cravings you might have. The chocolate must be a good brand and contain at least 70% cocoa solids or the finished sorbet will suffer as a result.

Lemon and almond cake

1 ½ cups blanched almonds • ½ cup all-purpose flour • 2 tbsp. grated lemon peel • 2 sticks unsalted butter, softened • 1 cup sugar • 3 eggs • 6 tbsp. fresh lemon juice • confectioners' sugar for dusting   **SERVES 10**

This is a moist crumbly cake that is delicious served warm just out of the oven with a spoonful of mascarpone on the side.

1. Preheat the oven to 300° F. Put the almonds in a food processor and blend until finely ground. Tip into a large mixing bowl and stir in the flour and lemon peel.

2. Wipe out the bowl of the food processor and add the butter and sugar. Blend until pale and smooth. With the motor running add the eggs and lemon juice and blend well.

3. Pour the egg mixture into the almond and flour mixture and fold in. Pour into an 8 ½-inch greased and lined springform pan. Bake until a skewer inserted into the middle of the cake comes out clean, 55 minutes to an hour. Leave 5 minutes in the pan then transfer to a plate and dust with confectioners' sugar.

chopping a mango

step 1 Put the mango on a board, with one rounded end toward you. Insert a chef's knife to find the stone then cut down the flesh closely to either side of it.

step 2 Take a smaller knife with a point and carefully run it round the edge of the two mango halves to loosen the flesh from the skin.

step 3 Being careful not to pierce the skin, take the point of the knife and score the flesh in a criss-cross pattern—about four cuts in both directions to give smallish cubes of flesh. Push up from the skin side so the pieces of mango pop up. Run a knife underneath the cubes to loosen them from the skin, then cut away, holding the mango over a bowl.

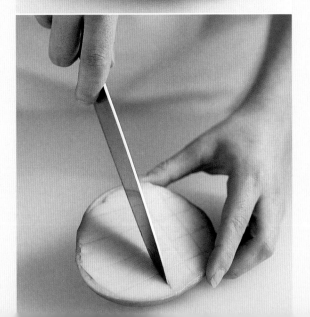

chopping a pineapple

step 1 Using a chef's knife, cut across the top to remove the leaves, and slice off the bottom to serve as a base. Holding the pineapple steady, carefully cut down to remove the skin.

step 2 Swap knives for this—a thin, serrated fruit knife is the most efficient. Carefully cut down the sides of the pineapple flesh to remove any eyes still remaining.

step 3 Back with the chef's knife, cut the pineapple in half, then cut each half into two pieces. Cut away the core from the center of each pineapple wedge.

Tropical fruit salad

**1-inch piece fresh ginger, peeled • 1 cup sugar • 1 star anise •
1 stick lemon grass • 2 kaffir lime leaves • 1 large mango •
1 papaya • 2 Asian pears • 1 melon, e.g., Ogen**

SERVES 4

1. Finely chop the ginger and put in a large saucepan with scant 2 cups water and sugar. Add the star anise, lemon grass, and lime leaves. Bring to a boil then simmer quite fiercely, 20 minutes, until the water has reduced and the liquid is quite syrupy. Remove the lime leaves and lemon grass. Allow to cool.

2. Cut the mango into cubes and put into a mixing bowl.

3. Halve the papaya lengthwise and scrape out the seeds. Peel carefully and cut into large cubes. Add to the mixing bowl.

4. Peel the Asian pears and remove the core. Slice quite thickly and stir in with the other fruit.

5. Halve the melon and scrape out the seeds. Quarter and remove the flesh from the rind. Cut into ½-inch slices. Put in the mixing bowl. Pour the syrup over the fruit and serve chilled.

Pineapple and scallion salsa

1 ripe pineapple, about 2 lbs. • 1 bunch scallions • 2 tbsp. olive oil • small bunch cilantro • 1 tbsp. fresh lemon juice

SERVES 4–6 as an accompaniment

This is a refreshing and zingy salsa, which livens up the dullest piece of meat.

1.Top and tail the pineapple with a chef's knife. Stand it on a board and cut down the sides to remove the skin.

2.Using a serrated fruit knife, cut out any eyes that remain in the flesh.

3.Cut into quarters lengthwise and slice out the core.

4.Finely dice the flesh and put in a mixing bowl.

5.Finely slice the scallions. Heat 1 tbsp. of the oil in a small pan and fry the scallions, 3–4 minutes. Cool then stir into the diced pineapple. Finely chop the cilantro and stir in with the lemon juice and remaining oil.

Rhubarb, orange, and ginger fool

6 stalks young rhubarb • 1 orange • ⅕ cup honey • 2 tbsp. brown sugar • 2 pieces
stem ginger in syrup (available in Asian markets) • 1 package vanilla pudding • ½ cup
heavy cream

SERVES 4–6

**This is a great way to use up the usual glut of rhubarb
through the summer and good enough to serve for a
dinner party. Serve with biscotti on the side.**

1. Wash and roughly chop the rhubarb and put in a saucepan.
Grate the peel from the orange and add to the rhubarb. Peel off the
skin and finely chop the flesh.

2. Add the honey and sugar to the rhubarb. Cover and cook until
the rhubarb is tender, 10–15 minutes. Pour into a large mixing bowl
and let cool. Finely chop the stem ginger and stir in.

3. Whisk the pudding and cream, and pour over the fruit. Chill until
ready to serve.

Chocolate and pecan pie

½ lb. ready-made pie crusts • 1½ cups pecans • 5 oz. unsweetened chocolate • 4 tbsp. unsalted butter • 3 large eggs • 1 cup golden brown sugar • ¾ cup maple syrup • 1 tbsp. all-purpose flour

SERVES 8–10

The pie is filled with a deliciously fudgy mixture of nuts, chocolate, and maple syrup.

1. Preheat the oven to 350° F. Line a 10-inch tart pan with the pie crust. Line with waxed paper and baking beans and bake blind, 20 minutes. Remove beans and paper. Reduce the oven temperature to 325° F.

2. Roughly chop three quarters of the pecans with a large knife and scatter over the cooked pie crust.

3. Roughly chop the chocolate and dice the butter and put in a bowl. Melt over a pan of gently simmering water or microwave on medium, 2 minutes. Stir and let cool.

4. Whisk together the eggs, sugar, and maple syrup. Stir in the cooled chocolate and fold in the flour. Pour into the pie crust.

5. Arrange the remaining nuts on top and bake until the center is just set, 50–55 minutes. Serve warm or cold with a dollop of whipped cream.

Orange terrine with citrus cream

5 large oranges • 2 ½ cups fresh orange juice • 4 tbsp. sugar • 1 ½ packages
unflavored gelatin • For the citrus cream • 2 tbsp. confectioners' sugar • 1 cup
half-and-half • 1 tbsp. orange flower water • 2 tsp. grated lemon peel • 2 tbsp.
fresh lemon juice • 2 tsp. grated lime peel

SERVES 6

This tanginess of this terrine is offset by the richness of the citrus cream. Many supermarkets and delis now sell orange flower water, but it can be omitted.

1. Cut the oranges into segments and put in a bowl.

2. Put the orange juice and sugar in a saucepan and heat to nearly boiling. Remove from the heat.

3. Add the gelatin to the heated orange juice and stir until dissolved. Allow to cool.

4. Lightly oil a 5 cup capacity terrine mold and place a layer of orange segments across the base. Continue to layer until three-quarters full. Pour the orange juice in and allow to set in the refrigerator, at least 6 hours. Turn out onto a flat serving plate.

5. For the citrus cream, just before serving sift the confectioners' sugar into the cream, add the orange flower water, and whip until it holds soft peaks. Stir in the lemon and lime peel, and the lemon juice. Serve with the terrine.

Top and tail the orange with a serrated fruit knife. Stand on one flat end and, following the curve of the orange, cut down the sides to remove the peel.

Hold the orange in one hand and carefully cut down in between the membranes, releasing the segments which should now be clean and clear of any membranes.

Passion fruit cheesecake

generous ½ cup (when processed) graham crackers • 6 tbsp. unsalted butter, melted • 9 passion fruit • 3⅓ packages cream cheese • ½ cup sugar • ½ cup half-and-half • 4 eggs, beaten • 3 egg yolks • 2 tsp. vanilla extract

SERVES 8–10

The fragrant flavor of the passion fruit raises this cheesecake to superstar status.

1. Put the crackers in a food processor and blend to fine crumbs. Pour in the melted butter and blend to mix. Spoon the crumbs into an 8½-inch springform pan and allow to set until hard in the fridge, 20 minutes. Cover the outside of the pan with a layer of foil. Preheat the oven to 325° F.

2. Cut six of the passion fruit in half. Put a sieve over a bowl and scrape the seeds into it. With the back of a wooden spoon extract as much juice from the seeds as possible.

3. Put the cream cheese, sugar, and cream in a food processor and blend until smooth. Pour in the eggs and egg yolks and blend again until well mixed. Add the vanilla extract and passion fruit juice and briefly blend. Pour the cheesecake mixture into the pan.

4. Put the pan in a bain-marie and bake, 1¼ hours. The foil around the pan will stop the water from leaking into the cheesecake, which should be just firm. Let cool in the oven for 10 minutes, then chill at least 3–4 hours. Once firm remove the sides of the pan. Scrape the seeds from the remaining passion fruit and pour over the cheesecake just before serving.

index

suppliers

Bed, Bath & Beyond
800-GO-BEYOND
www.bedbathandbeyond.com

Chef's
800-884-CHEF
www.chefscatalog.com

Crate & Barrel
800-967-6696
www.crateandbarrel.com

Dean & Deluca
877-826-9246
www.deandeluca.com

IKEA
610-834-1520
www.ikea.com

Pier 1 Imports
800-245-4595
www.pier1.com

Restoration Hardware
877-747-4671
www.restorationhardware.com

Target
888-304-4000
www.target.com

Williams-Sonoma
877-812-6235
www.williams-sonoma.com